Word

The Bible Day by Day
January–April 2011

HODDER &
STOUGHTON

First published in Great Britain in 2010 by Hodder & Stoughton
an Hachette UK company

Copyright © 2010 by The Salvation Army
International Headquarters, 101 Queen Victoria Street,
London EC4V 4EH

1

A CIP catalogue record for this title is available from the British Library

ISBN 978 1 444 70132 6

Typeset in Minion by Avon DataSet Ltd, Bidford on Avon, Warwickshire

Printed and bound in Great Britain
by Clays Ltd, St Ives plc

Hodder & Stoughton policy is to use papers that are natural, renewable
and recyclable products and made from wood grown in sustainable forests.
The logging and manufacturing processes are expected to conform to the
environmental regulations of the country of origin.

Hodder & Stoughton Ltd
338 Euston Road
London NW1 3BH

www.hodderfaith.com

Contents

Sundays

Psalm 119 affirms that God's Word is sure, pure and endures.

From the writer of *Words of Life*

This year a host of newly commissioned Salvation Army officers will come from the Ambassadors of Holiness Session. *Words of Life* archives show that a 1957 edition (then *The Soldier's Armoury*) devotes a month to the life of holiness. One of the 2003 editions features a study of Daniel, who was a sample of God's holiness. In this edition the guest series is about everyday holiness.

Annually there is a series surrounding Pentecost. But holiness is not only a seasonal emphasis of our faith. We find direct and indirect references to this facet of God's character throughout Scripture. The first temple's costly materials are meant to make a statement about the grandeur and majesty of the God of Israel and to encourage his people to revere and worship him. And we recall that God can use ordinary objects to teach us valuable lessons about who he is and what he can do with those who love and obey him. Further, guest writer Major Anita Caldwell suggests we reread holiness classics for down-to-earth advice.

In his first epistle, John helps us to understand the inestimable treasure believers have in Jesus, the Son of God, who radiates God's glory and expresses his very nature. Recognising whose we are should encourage us to live righteous lives and love one another. A writer of dark novels returned to faith in Christ after forty years of atheism. When interviewed about her more recent biblical novels and asked how returning to Christ had influenced her life, her new realisation was simply: 'It demands of me that I love people.'

When we join John in Revelation, his dream-like visions of heaven, like transient cherry blossoms, appear suddenly and must be appreciated before they fade. After glimpses of our heavenly home, God's final word to the reader is the grace of the Lord Jesus. The simple, selective, straightforward yet sublime writings of the elderly apostle take us right up through Easter as we turn to his unique Gospel and its emphasis on the doctrine of Jesus Christ as the Son of God. In the afterglow of Easter joy we spend a few days in quietness and hope, the fore glow of a glorious future.

Evelyn Merriam
New York, USA

Abbreviations

JBP *The New Testament in Modern English,* J. B. Phillips, Geoffrey Bles. © J. B. Philips, 1958, 1959, 1960, 1972. HarperCollins Publishers.

JMT *James Moffat Translation.* © 1922, 1924, 1925, 1926, 1935. Harper-Collins Publishers.

MSG *The Message,* Eugene H. Peterson. © 1993, 1994, 1995, 1996, 2000, 2001, 2002. Used by permission of NavPress Publishing Group.

NASB *New American Standard Bible.* © 1960, 1962, 1963, 1968, 1971, 1972, 1973, 1975, 1977, 1995 by The Lockman Foundation. Used by permission.

NEB *New English Bible.* © 1961, 1970, Oxford University Press.

NKJV *New King James Bible.* © 1982 by Thomas Nelson, Inc. Used by permission. All rights reserved.

NLT *New Living Translation.* © Tyndale House Publishers, 1996, 1998.

SASB *The Song Book of The Salvation Army.* © 1986 The General of The Salvation Army.

TNIV *Today's New International Version.* © 2004 by International Bible Society. Used by permission of Hodder & Stoughton Publishers, an Hachette UK Company. All rights reserved. 'TNIV' is a registered trademark of Biblica.

Christ our King

'He is before all things, and in him all things hold together' (v. 17).

Christmas decorations and carols are being tucked away. As we greet one another with 'Happy New Year!' and replace the worn 2010 calendars with fresh 2011s, we might think of long-range plans in our work or for privately cherished dreams. However, there's one event no one can yet mark on the church calendar. As we live each day to please the Lord, we'll be ready for the day, should this be the year of Christ our King's return.

In her poems of threefold praise to Christ our Lord, based on today's Scripture portion, retired Salvation Army officer Lieut-Colonel Marlene Chase[1] describes 'The Cosmic Christ', 'The Incarnate Christ' and 'The Triumphant King'. The third encourages us and helps set the tone for our New Year:

The Triumphant King

Down the years his blood has flowed,
a river wide enough, deep enough
to consume the wild rages of sin.
Beneath its pure waves men have plunged
to find themselves alive as he:
Alive to love that shimmers, dances
and compels their homeward hearts.
Once more he leaves the hearth of Heaven
to guide his children home.
This time, no mewling, cooing Babe,
but the King emblazoned with glory
and dazzling in holy light.
See him recall the four winds,
coil the oceans in his robe,
wrap up stars and galaxies in his train.
Fashioned in purity and shining joy,
his Bride rises to meet the Lord!

P – Pe

*'The unfolding of your words gives light; it gives understanding
to the simple' (v. 130).*

As we continue from last year with Psalm 119, our key verse presents
several word pictures. The phrase, 'unfolding of your words', may
remind us of an intricate origami design. If we unfold it step by step, we
discover how it became the final object. Or we might think of a flower that
unfolds in response to the sun and displays its full beauty. Unfolding the
paper design brings understanding and the unfolding blossom gives
pleasure.

Another metaphor comes to mind as we read the verse in *The Message*:
'Break open your words, let your light shine out.' Instead of something
unfolding, it's something broken open, such as a coconut.

Even better, think of Gideon's 300 select men who surprised the
Midianite camp at night with startling sights and sounds. Not only did they
simultaneously blow trumpets and shout, but also they shattered the
pitchers in which they had concealed lit torches. The blaze of light that
encircled the camp confounded the enemy, but lit the way for the troop
who shouted 'the sword of the LORD and of Gideon' (Judges 7:18, *NKJV*);
certainly an apt metaphor for the word.

The psalmist finishes verse 130 stating that God's words give ordinary
people understanding. When some versions use the word 'simple' at the
end of the verse, they don't mean the foolish or the simpleminded, but
those who are teachable. We take heart.

In verse 131 the writer describes his keen desire for God's word as
breathlessly panting for air. If our desire is to know God's will through his
word, we too can confidently ask that God would turn to us, have mercy
on us, direct our behaviour, make us sure-footed, keep us from sin's
dominion, free us from the oppression of others and give us a sense of his
favour. Then as each day of the new year unfolds and we open our Bibles,
we will find light.

Solomon's Splendid Reign

2 Chronicles 1–9

Introduction

We visit part of another Old Testament book which *Words of Life* has not commented on in recent years – 2 Chronicles. Some passages are unique to 2 Chronicles, but many details are also found in the parallel accounts in 1 Kings 1–11. While the reigns of about twenty kings of Judah are described in 2 Chronicles, a quarter of the chapters, the nine we visit, are devoted to one king – Solomon.

Writing in the time of Ezra, the chronicler was probably attached to the restored temple. He would have insight into the purpose and function of worship and its importance to the nation. Of the chapters dealing with Solomon's reign, two thirds detail the temple; 'It is evident that the building of the Temple is more important to the Chronicler than the biography of the builder.'[2]

The opulence of the temple is dazzling. Yet we recall that Jesus warns another generation not to be blinded by the gold of their temple, but to recognise what it represents and the more essential values of worship and its true object (Matthew 23:16–22).

We sometimes dismiss Solomon because of things that happened later in his career when he acted as though he was without accountability and ignored the counsel of Scripture. But we should also remember what went well when he was following the Lord's ways. Solomon's name means peaceable, perfect, or one who recompenses.

The Gospels record a couple of times when Jesus refers to Solomon's reputation for grandeur or wisdom. Once when religious leaders demanded evidence of Jesus' credentials he reminded them: 'On Judgment Day, the Queen of Sheba will come forward and bring evidence that will condemn this generation, because she traveled from a far corner of the earth to listen to wise Solomon. Wisdom far greater than Solomon's is right in front of you, and you quibble over "evidence"' (Matthew 12:42, *MSG*).

We briefly revisit Solomon's splendid reign, but rejoice to know the ultimate and eternal wisdom and power of God – Christ Jesus.

A New King's First Action

'Solomon son of David established himself firmly over his kingdom, for the LORD *his God was with him and made him exceedingly great' (v. 1).*

When we commented on the final chapter of 1 Chronicles last July, we noted that before King David died he formally handed over the throne and the kingdom to one of his sons, Solomon. He charged both Solomon and the people to follow God's commands, gave Solomon the clear, detailed, Spirit-inspired instructions about building the temple, and emphasised the enormity of the task of building a sanctuary for the Lord.

David gave a magnanimous donation that inspired his people to generosity, and then rejoiced in a public prayer of praise to God. A massive animal sacrifice wrapped up the dedication ceremony, after which the people enjoyed a feast together before the Lord. Solomon was publicly re-anointed king and Zadok as high priest.

The first verse of 2 Chronicles shows the continuation of the Davidic line as, under God's blessing, Solomon establishes himself in his royal role. At the outset the new king speaks to military, judicial and other leaders as well as heads of families and leads them to the tent of meeting at Gibeon for worship.

David had moved the ark of the covenant to Jerusalem, but the rest of the tabernacle fashioned in the wilderness was at Gibeon. This included the bronze altar (Exodus 38:1–7) made by God's chosen craftsman, Bezalel, according to the divine design (Exodus 31:2–5). Perhaps Solomon recognises that it is the presence of the Lord that is essential and chooses a location where God's presence is symbolised by the altar.

On that altar, first used in the days of Moses, Solomon offered 1,000 burnt offerings. He doesn't upstage the sacrifice his father authorised at the public transfer of the kingdom (more than 3,000 animals), but offering 1,000 animal sacrifices ties his reign to that of his father.

When we are at the start of a new chapter of life – a position, a place to live, a commitment or other challenging responsibility – is our first impulse to worship the Lord sacrificially?

More than He Asks

'Yes, give me wisdom and knowledge as I come and go among this people – for who on his own is capable of leading these, your glorious people?' (v. 10, MSG)

After the drama and exhilaration of public worship, and with the tang of the smoke from 1,000 sacrifices still in the air, that night Solomon has a personal encounter with the Lord. In 1 Kings 3:5 we're told that it is through a dream. Both 1 Kings and 2 Chronicles say that God asks Solomon to name what he wants.

Solomon first acknowledges that he comes to the throne because of God's kindness to his father, David. He has grown up in the shadow of his father's reign, but until now without its weighty responsibility. So next he admits he knows the enormity of his task – ruling a great and numerous people (v. 9). He even says: 'But I am only a little child and do not know how to carry out my duties' (1 Kings 3:7). Some commentators estimate that Solomon was probably no more than age twenty-five when he began to reign.

The young king perceptively realises he needs discernment to govern well and to distinguish right from wrong, so he asks God for wisdom and knowledge. God is pleased. The young man could have made a selfish request for long life, wealth, fame or even the demise of his enemies, but he doesn't.

The Lord commends Solomon and promises him the gift of unparalleled wisdom and discernment. Additionally God promises him the extra unsought blessings of riches, honour and unequalled status among rulers. He gives him a challenge that comes with its own reward: 'And if you walk in my ways and obey my statutes and commands as David your father did, I will give you a long life' (1 Kings 3:14).

Solomon may be overwhelmed with gratitude. His response is to return to Jerusalem, stand before the ark of the covenant, offer further sacrifices and then give a banquet for his court (1 Kings 3:15). The new king humbly worships God and generously extends hospitality to others. These two characteristics still remain a complementary pair.

Building with Purpose

'The temple I am going to build will be great, because our God is greater than all other gods' (v. 5).

Almost parenthetically, at the end of 2 Chronicles 1 the writer tells us that Solomon accumulates horses and chariots and keeps them in designated chariot cities. He also amasses great wealth: 'The king made silver and gold as common in Jerusalem as stones, and cedar as plentiful as sycamore-fig trees in the foothills' (2 Chronicles 1:15). Such unmistakable evidences of power are impressive.

Although these advances must have taken considerable planning, time and effort, the chronicler only mentions them in passing (1:14–17). It's not that he thinks they are unimportant, but he hastens to what he considers the most significant aspect of Solomon's reign – constructing the temple.

Solomon assigns a massive workforce to quarry and carry stone before applying to the king of Tyre for materials and a skilled superintendent for the legendary building project first proposed by King David. The expert master craftsman should be able to handle proficiently both precious and rugged metals, work with fabric and do decorative embroidery and woodcarving. It sounds like the job description of the artisan Bezalel a couple of hundred years earlier. God chose and filled him with his Spirit, with wisdom, knowledge and ability to make the artistic motifs that the divine design for the tabernacle required, and to teach others how to do so as well (see Exodus 35).

Solomon also requests timber from the valued cedar, cypress and algum trees – rare and durable woods – and promises to send assistants for Tyre's skilled loggers, and substantial food supplies.

Solomon's message to the king of Tyre reveals his vision for the celebrated edifice. He does not focus on the temple's size; rather he focuses on its purpose. The temple would be erected to the name of the Lord, would be a place dedicated to sacrifice and worship, and would be great because of God's greatness. Shouldn't we likewise purposely build all, even our lives, to the glory of our great God?

Man of Many Parts

'He is experienced in all kinds of engraving and can execute any design given to him. He will work with your craftsmen and with those of my lord, David your father' (v. 14).

Except perhaps for Christmas cards we hope to enjoy again unhurriedly, many of us will have packed away everything related to Christmas and begun a new year. Yet in some Christian traditions it is Epiphany (today) that marks the official end of Christmas. It is celebrated as the day the Magi visited Christ. It looks ahead to the mission of the Church to the world in light of the nativity.

Nearly 1,000 years before the Church is born, Solomon builds the first temple. King Hiram replies to Solomon's request in writing. It is remarkable that nearly 3,000 years ago these kings exchanged correspondence. Some ancient civilisations thought Hiram's and Solomon's kingdoms less sophisticated, yet Hiram and Solomon were literate.

Hiram says he's sending Solomon a man with roots in Tyre and Israel, Hurum-abi. The 1 Kings 7 account says his mother was from the tribe of Naphtali (settled adjacent to the mountains of Lebanon) whereas the 2 Chronicles 2 account says she was from the tribe of Dan (which settled further south along the coast, adjacent to the tribe of Benjamin's portion, which included Jerusalem). There may be confusion in the records, or the woman may have been the daughter of parents from two different tribes. The king shows wisdom in selecting an artisan with this background.

Hiram agrees to use Solomon's workforce, cut the trees in the north and float them in rafts by sea more than 100 miles south to the port of Joppa (v. 16). Significantly, the trees are cut from near the Naphtali region and shipped from Tyre to the Dan region.

Not only is Hurum-abi a qualified and experienced master artisan, but Hiram is confident that he can work with Solomon's craftsmen as well as David's. The master can work with people and respects others' abilities, including those of an older generation. Might we ask God's Spirit to so enable us as well?

A Gold Standard

'Give unto the LORD the glory due to his name; worship the LORD in the beauty of holiness' (Psalm 29:2, NKJV).

So in the fourth year of Solomon's reign, in the springtime when the earth responds to the ever-lengthening days, the work on the temple begins. Solomon knows it is to be situated on the land David purchased by divine direction. First, David built an altar to the Lord and afterwards declared the place would be the future site for the house of the Lord (1 Chronicles 21:18, 19, 25, 26 and 22:1).

The temple's foundation, given in cubits, is about ninety feet by thirty feet. A cubit is a measure from the tip of a man's fingers to his elbow. In verse 3 the chronicler mentions that the standard of cubit measure Solomon uses is from the 'old standard' – from the times of Moses when the cubit equalled about eighteen inches.

When the Israelites return from captivity in Babylon, they use the Babylonian measure, which varies from the 'old' cubit. Since the books of Chronicles are written after the captivity, for accuracy the writer wants to distinguish which standard Solomon uses. Perhaps he connects something essential about Solomon's building with the tabernacle for which Moses also used the 'old standard' of measure. In any case, the temple's rectangular design is a durable form of the earlier portable tabernacle plan and twice its size.

The workers' approach seems reverent and deliberate. The massive blocks of stone are cut to measure at the quarry so that at the site no heavy iron tools are needed and noise is reduced (1 Kings 6:7). Inside the structure of stone and specially prepared rare timber, Solomon panels the sanctuary with pine and adds elaborate decorative carvings.

He covers almost every surface except the marble floor with gold. He even uses heavy gold nails or bolts (2 Chronicles 2 5–9). The Parvaim gold may come from the distant east or be gold with a warm reddish hue. Gold reflects and amplifies any glimmer of light.

Gold reminds us of the Magi's gift to Christ the King and John's many references to gold in the heavenly city – all symbols of the worthiness of our holy, eternal and matchless God. Praise him!

Designed to Declare

'But you are a chosen people . . . that you may declare the praises of him
who called you out of darkness into his wonderful light' (1 Peter 2:9).

Even though by today's standards the temple Solomon built might not be impressive in size, its craftsmanship was of the highest level. Although the tabernacle in the wilderness took six months to complete and the temple seven years and six months, if we compare the plans for the temple with those of its precursor (Exodus 25–27), we note a number of parallels in the divine designs.

The proportion of both measures three times as long as wide. They both have an outer court, a main room or sanctuary and an 'inner house', *debir*, or Holy of Holies. In the temple the Holy of Holies is a thirty-foot gold-overlaid cube. There is a pair of cherubim in both.

The smaller cherubim in the tabernacle are part of the golden covering of the ark of the covenant and, facing each other, look toward the mercy seat with upward-spanning wings overshadowing it. They are of hammered gold and sit at the ends of the ark, which is less than four feet long.

In the temple the cherubim, each with a fifteen-foot wingspan, stand on the floor side-by-side and wall-to-wall, facing the main sanctuary. These fifteen-foot-tall angels are made of olive wood overlaid with gold (1 Kings 6:23). They will overshadow the ark.

In both structures a fine linen curtain decorated with sky-blue, deep scarlet and rich purple thread and embroidered cherubim hangs at the entrance to the Holy of Holies. Unique to the temple is a pair of immense emblems – pillars which stand outside its entrance. They're bronze and elaborately decorated with chains that look like enormous necklaces from which hang 200 pomegranates.

The pillars are named Jakin ('He that strengthens and makes steadfast') and Boaz ('In strength and stability'). They stand for David's kingdom being established and for Boaz, David's great-grandfather and the patriarch of the family of kings from the house of Judah. If even pillars can remind people of God's enablement and goodness, how much more should our lives so 'declare . . . him who called you' (1 Peter 2:9)?

On to Perfect Love

'Therefore, leaving the discussion of the elementary principles of Christ,
let us go on to perfection' (Hebrews 6:1, NKJV).

We first comment on a verse from last Sunday's reading. After the psalmist shows a thoroughgoing commitment to God's word and way, he laments: 'I cry rivers of tears because nobody's living by your book!' (Psalm 119:136, *MSG*). Like the writer of Lamentations, he expresses compassion over the sins and downfall of others (Jeremiah 8:22–9:1). This attitude stands in contrast with the psalmist's previous resentment towards those who disregard God's law.

His compassionate attitude follows his plea to be free from any form of sin (Psalm 119:133). Some have called this an Old Testament prayer for New Testament perfection (such as Paul expresses in Romans). Perhaps the psalmist sees how limited his own knowledge of God's way has been and for the first time is concerned about those who disobey it at their peril.

Holiness teacher Samuel Logan Brengle also knew overwhelming compassion shortly after coming to personally know the blessing of holiness on today's date in 1885. He says he saw his selfishness and un-holiness in contrast with Christ's selflessness and holiness. He surrendered to the Holy Spirit's cleansing and trusted the promise of 1 John 1:9. Peace came to his heart.

He immediately testified to his experience in conversations and in his next sermon using today's key verse. 'This public confession helped him confirm the inward impression of his experience. He stepped out on faith and there was no turning back.'[3]

Brengle writes of what happened two mornings later when he was overwhelmed with divine love while reading words of Jesus:

I walked out over Boston Common before breakfast, weeping for joy and praising God . . . In that hour I knew Jesus and I loved him till it seemed my heart would break with love. I loved the sparrows, I loved the dogs, I loved the horses, I loved the little urchins on the streets, I loved the strangers who hurried past me, I loved the heathen – I loved the whole world.[4]

Totally Committed

*'That completed the work King Solomon did on the Temple of GOD.
He then brought in the holy offerings of his father David, the silver
and the gold and the artefacts. He placed them all in the treasury
of God's Temple' (5:1, MSG).*

Besides constructing the temple, under King Solomon's direction, master craftsman Huram-abi also oversees producing its furnishings. Some pieces, such as the bronze entrance pillars, the altar for sacrifice and the laver, are massive. The pillars are twenty-seven feet tall, the altar on which to burn sacrifices is thirty feet long and wide and fifteen feet tall. The laver for the priests to wash in holds thousands of gallons of water.

The bronze objects are cast at a national foundry in the plains of the Jordan River near where the Jabbok River enters it (1 Kings 7:46). There the mixture of sand and clay essential for casting such immense objects is abundant. Transporting the huge objects from the Jordan to Jerusalem would arrest attention. Even the sites such as the foundry, the quarry and the forest which contribute to the temple project are impressive.

As the chapter details, the altar of incense, lamp stands and tables, lavers for rinsing the sacrifices and their stands, door coverings and the essential temple utensils down to pots, shovels, sprinkling bowls, wick trimmers and decorative designs are either made of polished bronze or gold as appropriate and designated.

In today's market, the amount of gold Solomon uses would be worth more than US$75 billion. That profusion is probably additional to the gold David set aside. Our key verse says that when the temple is complete, Solomon places his father's dedicated provision of silver and gold in the treasury of God's temple. Solomon apparently raises or bears most of the temple's expenses himself. It is rightly called Solomon's temple.

Solomon's equivalent of a diary, project notes and cheque book would reveal how invested he is in accomplishing the mission the Lord gives him. What do our schedules, plans and finances reveal?

More than Gold

'The glory of the LORD *filled the temple of God' (v. 14).*

A final design for One World Trade Center in New York was unveiled in 2006. Some time this year the final beam will be placed and the building will be ready for occupancy by 2013. For many whose lives were directly or indirectly affected by the tragedy of 9/11, the seven years of construction to replace the felled North and South Towers must seem a very long time.

Elsewhere, between the time in 2005 when London was chosen as host of the 2012 Olympic Games and the opening of those Summer Olympics, numerous sites have been under construction. Those affected may have adjusted to detours and inconveniences, but will be relieved when the venues and infrastructure projects are completed and the Games begin.

The seven and a half years' construction work on Solomon's temple ends and the temple is finished. It's the time of year of the annual Feast of Booths. Solomon calls all the leaders of the people together for a feast of dedication to formalise the completion of the temple and to celebrate.

Using prescribed carrying poles, the Levites transfer the ark, the symbol of the presence of God, to the new temple. In keeping with the importance of the event, Solomon and all those assembled offer innumerable sacrifices before the ark (v. 6). All the priests consecrate themselves for this day and some of them carefully place the ark in the Holy of Holies.

With Asaph leading the way, as he had when David brought the ark to Jerusalem, the Levite musicians play their instruments. The trumpets alone number 120. When the singers join in song to the Lord, 'He is good; his love endures forever', it must make a tremendous and memorable paean of praise. The glory of the Lord fills the temple. This beautifies it more than all the gold within. Even priestly service ceases. God is present.

The construction disruption has been worthwhile. The ark and the people have a permanent home in the Promised Land. The Lord is with this generation and they know it first hand. By his Spirit, the Lord confirms his presence to us today as well.

Where He Dwells

'But now I have chosen Jerusalem for my Name to be there' (v. 6).

Throughout the year we observe numerous types of clouds, portending turbulent or fair weather. But when Solomon refers to the cloud that fills the temple he doesn't need to explain its significance. The glory of the Lord appears to God's people in like form throughout their history.

When they leave Egypt, the Lord guides them by his cloud pillar (Exodus 13:21). When, less than two months into their journey, the people complain about having no meat, Moses and Aaron summon the whole community to stand before the Lord. When they look towards the desert, they see the glory of the Lord appearing in a cloud (Exodus 16:10).

Later, the Lord calls to Moses from within the cloud on Mount Sinai. To the Israelites below, the cloud seems to be a fire on top of the mountain. Moses enters the cloud and stays on the mountain for forty days (Exodus 24:16–18). He receives the initial commandments and detailed instructions for the tabernacle.

Before the tabernacle is built, Moses pitches a tent outside the camp which he calls 'the tent of meeting'. When he enters it, the people watch from the doors of their own tents as the pillar of cloud stands at its entrance and God communes with Moses. When they see the cloud, the people worship (Exodus 33:10).

On the day the tabernacle is finished, the cloud covers it. At night it looks like fire (Exodus 40:34–38). Adam Clarke's commentary on the Old Testament tells us: 'The cloud descending at these times and at none others was a full proof that it was miraculous, and a pledge of the divine presence. It was beyond the power of human art to counterfeit such an appearance.'

Now at the temple's dedication, after the cloud filled the sanctuary, King Solomon turns to bless the people, and then praises God for fulfilling his promises, guiding his people to the present moment and allowing David's dream for a temple to come to pass through his son. He reminds the people that it is all of God's choosing (v. 6). God still dwells and works in the midst of his willing people.

13

In This Very Place

'Can it be that God will actually move into our neighbourhood? Why, the cosmos itself isn't large enough to give you breathing room, let alone this Temple I've built' (v. 18, MSG).

After blessing the people in front of the temple and still in plain sight of the assembly, Solomon turns from facing them to facing the altar. He stands on a seven-foot-square platform in the outer court. He's elevated about four or five feet above the ground. People can see him from wherever they are in the crowd. But when he kneels to pray, perhaps most don't see the man but just the back of his outstretched arms as he prays.

His prayer is something like this: There is no God like you. You keep covenant with your people who follow you from the bottom of their hearts. You have kept your promises, please keep it up. Is it possible you will dwell in this temple when even the heavens can't contain you?

In this vein, if he'd had a Salvation Army songbook he might have led in a verse of Samuel Medley's song:

> Thy presence and thy glories, Lord,
> Fill all the realms of space;
> O come, and at thy people's prayer
> Now consecrate this place.
>
> (*SASB* 946)

Solomon continues: But hear my prayer today. And please stay attentive day and night to our prayers when your people pray towards this place you promised to dignify with your name. Listen, hear and forgive us.

Solomon is confident that God can hear and help his sincere followers who come to him on his terms. He's aware that such followers need more than God's blessings or even his listening ear. They need something which only a just and loving God can provide: grace and forgiveness. Believers know it through acceptance of God's love and salvation revealed in Christ. Let's take time to remember where God's grace has reached us.

For Their Own Good

'That they will fear you and walk in your ways' (v. 31).

At the dedication of the temple, Solomon invokes God's continued care for his people and asks that when they are penitent God will forgive. Then the king's prayer expands to detail further scenarios he considers likely. His prayer takes the form of 'if this happens, and we turn to you; then please do this'. He lists seven cases in which God's intervention, judgment and mercy would be indispensable. The passage is parallel to the one in 1 Kings 8:31–50.

The first petition deals with unsubstantiated accusations. Solomon asks that when the accused gives an oath of testimony on his own behalf that the Lord will uncover the truth, so justice would be done. Next, if the people are defeated because of sin and then ask God's forgiveness, Solomon asks that the Lord will forgive them, bring them victory and return them to their land of inheritance.

Third, if the people stop following God's way and are disciplined through drought, but then turn from sin and ask for forgiveness in the name of the Lord, the king asks that the Lord will forgive them and teach them the right way again.

If calamities of various kinds come because of sin, Solomon asks that when any of God's people knows the plague of their own heart and admits it and prays sincerely, then the Lord will hear and forgive them individually so that each would thereafter personally fear God and want to follow his ways.

As for those foreigners or strangers who are attracted to God's greatness and come seeking him, Solomon prays that when such seekers pray God will hear and answer them so that word of his name and power will spread throughout the world.

The sixth petition is for God's help and blessing in time of battle, but only when it is undertaken by God's commission. The song 'I'll go in the strength of the Lord' (*SASB* 734) comes to mind. Finally, the king prays that when sin leads to the nation's captivity, and the people have a change of heart, confess their sin and wholeheartedly turn back to God, God will forgive his people.

Reflexive Praise

'He is good; his love endures for ever' (v. 3).

The conclusion of Solomon's dedicatory prayer (vv. 40–42) begins as the parallel portion in 1 Kings 8 does, asking God to be attentive to the prayers of his people. But there are a few notable additions in Chronicles which seem to be similar to verses in Psalm 132. That unattributed psalm might have been written by David, by returning exiles or by Solomon himself.

If Solomon was the writer, the chronicler might be quoting some of the king's own words which he could have used on more than one occasion. The chronicler would have connected the Davidic line and the significance of the Messianic psalm with the dedication.

The chronicler records Solomon asking that the Lord come to his resting place (Psalm 132:8). He asks that the Lord's priests be clothed with salvation or righteousness and his saints rejoice in his goodness (Psalm 132:9). The king desires more than that God's servants wear appropriate attire for service – splendid white linen – they must also know the splendour of clean hearts and minds; more than the *symbols* of holy service, the *substance* of personal holiness. God still desires a holy people who delight in him.

Finally, Solomon requests that God does not reject him as king – a request rooted in the great steadfast love God promised to David and his descendants (Psalm 132:10, 11). The Lord shows approval of Solomon's sincere prayer and sends fire to consume the burnt offerings, and his glory to fill the temple.

The people are overwhelmed with the miraculous sight and they all kneel, as the king has, to worship God. They thank God in unison with familiar words from the psalms: 'He is good; his love endures for ever.' If this is the title of the song or psalm they repeat, it could be Psalm 136 in which the phrase is the refrain in all its verses.

How do we respond when we have a sense of God's overwhelming holiness, glory or presence? Often it is through wonderful words of Scripture or song we've learnt by heart. What is on the tips of our tongues as we prepare to worship the Lord tomorrow?

T – *Tsadhe*

'Righteous are you, O LORD, and your laws are right' (v. 137).

God's ways and expectations delight the psalmist and command his respect. He recognises that everything good and right about God's ways that he loves emanates from God's own righteous nature, so he states that first, at the start of our key verse. God's essential righteousness, purity and holiness are foundational.

God's nature pervades all that comes from him, including his promises. In verse 140 the writer states: 'Thy promises are tried and true, thy servant loves them' (*JMT*). 'Your word is very pure; therefore your servant loves it' (*NKJV*). The word translated as 'tried and true' and 'very pure' is literally 'refined'. We think of highly refined, valuable 24-carat gold.

In times of economic instability, the value of gold strengthens as people invest in it more and more. Because some countries hoard it in reserves and because of the dwindling number of new sources of ore, in recent years its value has risen to an all-time high. Misers in literature and life hoard their gold to gain power and control, but never have quite enough to satisfy them. No wonder misery comes from the same root word.

God's gold – his word – does not change in value; it is always priceless and it is available. It is worth both amassing and sharing. God's absolute righteousness, purity, truth and faithfulness gleam through Scripture. We see them best in Jesus. Adam Clarke's comment on verse 140 reminds us that God's word is not only pure, but it purifies.

We pray with The Salvation Army's poet-General, Albert Orsborn:

> Let the beauty of Jesus be seen in me,
> All his wonderful passion and purity,
> O thou Spirit divine, all my nature refine,
> Till the beauty of Jesus be seen in me.
>
> (*SASB* chorus 77)

Memorable Days

'Then at the end of the celebration, Solomon sent the people home.
They were all joyful and glad because the LORD had been so good to
David and to Solomon and to his people Israel' (v. 10, NLT).

The time chosen for the dedication of the temple is nearly a year after its completion. Solomon may want it to take place at the most appropriate time, just prior to the time Israel gathers for the Feast of Tabernacles or Booths, a festival around harvest time that all male Israelites must attend. A vast assembly from throughout Israel attends Solomon's back-to-back week-long celebrations (vv. 8, 9).

Some scholars think that, additionally, the temple's dedication was in one of the Jubilee years. If so, that would make it particularly memorable. Commensurate with the occasion, they have antiphonal music from a full complement of dedicated musicians from the guilds David had organised (v. 6). Perhaps Solomon recalls his father first involving the musicians in the dedication procession when he brought the ark to Jerusalem.

Now King Solomon and the people offer an immense number of sacrifices – 142,000 animals. There isn't enough room on the bronze altar for all these offerings, so a place in the centre of the court is consecrated especially for the purpose.

One commentator suggests that this may have been the rock on which David built an altar and sacrificed burnt and peace offerings when he purchased the land from the Jebusite (1 Chronicles 21:26). On that occasion the Lord answered David's prayer with a sacrifice-consuming fire. Then in faith David declared: 'The house of the LORD God is to be here and also the altar of burnt offering for Israel' (1 Chronicles 22:1).

After two weeks, when Solomon sends the people home, they go on their way full of joy for what God has done. They'll long remember meaningful worship and these shared days of exceptional scents, sights and sounds at the temple. As God's living temples, when our hearts are filled with reverence for God's greatness, we too can joyfully praise him and seek to reflect his glory.

If . . . Then

'If you live in my presence . . . pure in heart and action' (v. 17, MSG).

Everything regarding the temple and its dedication is complete. After the exhilaration of public worship the crowds disperse. Now once again the Lord appears to Solomon at night. The Lord's appearance reassures the king that God is aware of his work and prayers. This time he acknowledges the king's prayer, gives further blessing and cautions him.

In connection with the dedication of the temple, when Solomon prayed that God would hear and answer his people's prayers, the king stipulated that this should be conditional on their turning to God on his terms. God now uses a similar 'if . . . then' conditional form with the king, first regarding the people, then regarding the king himself.

The Lord says that during moral and spiritual decline and ensuing unrelenting trouble in the land: 'If . . . my people, my God-defined people, respond by humbling themselves, praying, seeking my presence, and turning their backs on their wicked lives, I'll be there ready for you: I'll listen from heaven, forgive their sins, and restore their land to health' (v. 14, *MSG*).

We may wonder why in verses 17–22 God speaks so explicitly to Solomon about obeying his commands and warns against following other gods. He even counsels that his lapses will result in calamity for the people of Israel. Perhaps it is in response to a hint of the king's lack of wisdom, skewed thinking and misconceptions about spiritual things. In his prayer Solomon seemed to shift the responsibility for his behaviour to God: 'O LORD God, do not turn away the face of your anointed' (2 Chronicles 6:42, *NKJV*).

In spite of Solomon's privileged upbringing, his strong start as ruler and God's specific warnings and promises, the king isn't watchful and gradually slips into the habit of acting as though he is exempt from obeying God. Late in life he reaps the sad consequences of his behaviour and knows deep regret. The truly wise choose to follow God's way from the start and, if detoured, quickly return to it.

A Splendid Kingdom

'Your kingdom is an everlasting kingdom, and your dominion endures through all generations' (Psalm 145:13).

Although we sometimes focus on Solomon's later years of decline, his life was not a complete ruin. He is on a par with many other great minds of his time. Solomon exhibits skilful administrative ability. His first twenty years as king are chiefly devoted to building the temple and his own palace. He also builds parks, reservoirs, stables and vineyards. 'Solomon built impulsively and extravagantly – wherever he fancied' (v. 6, *MSG*).

He ensures that the daily burnt offerings are made at the altar and observes the three prescribed annual festivals. He also keeps the full complement of priests on duty for worship (vv. 12–15).

Solomon not only learned his religious roots from his youth when he possibly had Nathan as his tutor, but also developed wide interests: from botany to zoology, writing to music. He becomes a diplomat and business-man. He raises a royal navy. He is privileged and gifted and for a while uses his gifts wisely in pursuit of excellence. Solomon acquires fame, fortune, power, pleasure.

Never again would there be such grandeur in Israel. News of it still circulated hundreds of years later so that, without explanation, Jesus could refer to Solomon's splendour and to those such as the queen who travelled great distances to listen to his wisdom. Jesus didn't deprecate Solomon's splendour, but elevated the elegant beauty of God's creation, even in something as simple as a wildflower (Matthew 6:29).

The kingdom knows peace during Solomon's forty-year reign. As great as Solomon's kingdom may be, even at its most glittering, it pales when compared with the kingdom of our King.

In Psalm 145 Solomon's father commends the worthiness of 'God the King', his greatness, his name, deeds, majesty, power, goodness, righteous-ness, compassion and the glorious splendour of his enduring dominion and eternal kingdom. Through Christ we're citizens of that truly splendid kingdom. Hallelujah!

'Loved by the Lord'

*'Kings came from all over the world to be with Solomon and get in
on the wisdom God had given him' (v. 23, MSG).*

The visit of the Queen of Sheba, possibly on a diplomatic trade mission,
points out Solomon's most significant achievements: wisdom and
wealth. What the queen sees confirms the reports that she's heard about
Solomon's greatness. What impresses her is a combination of the king's
wisdom, royal buildings, meals, officials, well-dressed attendants and the
offerings made at the temple.

Now that she sees for herself and believes, she's overwhelmed. The
queen shows discernment when she says to Solomon: 'Blessed be your
GOD who has taken such a liking to you, making you king. Clearly, GOD's
love for Israel is behind this, making you king to keep a just order and
nurture a God-pleasing people' (v. 8, *MSG*).

The queen presents lavish gifts from her country: tons of gold, countless
sacks of spices and precious stones. Solomon reciprocates by giving her
whatever she asks for so that she takes away more than she brings and
returns home satisfied on many levels.

As the chronicler concludes the record of Solomon he ignores incidents
recorded elsewhere (especially in 1 Kings 11): the decline of the nation; the
king's broken health; his defiance of God's ways; his idolatry and his many
wives; God's anger with him which leads to a sharp, solemn warning; the
king's extravagance at the expense of his people; and the treachery of his
adversaries – Hadad, Rezon and Jeroboam. Besides what his tutors taught
him formally, Solomon learnt about life from observing pride, selfishness,
deception, rape, murder and rebellion in his family. Messages of deviation
from God's ways no doubt filled his subconscious mind.

Yet this son of David and Bathsheba was loved of the Lord who even
sent word through Nathan the prophet that they should name him
Jedidiah, meaning 'Loved by the Lord' (2 Samuel 12:25). He had every
opportunity through his choices to own that name. His father learnt
personally that God is a God of fresh starts. So we too may choose to live
as those who are 'Loved by the Lord'.

Becoming Worthy Vessels

Introduction

Pottery, the ceramic ware potters produce, broadly includes earthenware, stoneware and porcelain as well as offshoots and derivatives. It starts as some form of clay which, when fired, can become impermeable, strong, durable and heat-resistant. Only after firing is it pottery, yet without a potter there would be no pottery.

A friend gave me a blue-and-white Dutch tile reproduction of Jan Luyken's 1694 engraving, *De Pottebakker* (The Potter). The work of the potter through the centuries and the process of transforming clay to pottery fascinates me, and over the next days we'll examine a few of the terms associated with this enduring art form.

The metaphor of the potter and the clay is well known in Scripture and has been used and commented on by many Christian writers. In preparing this segment, I've especially appreciated *Impressions in Clay* by porcelain doll sculptor Wendy Lawton[5] and *Worthy Vessels* by Nell L. Kennedy.[6]

Also, a number of years ago I read an article in which a Salvation Army officer drew practical lessons from symmetrical and free-form pottery. Before becoming an officer in the United Kingdom, Major Keith Wallis (who has a first-class honours degree in ceramics), taught pottery at secondary school and college levels. He recently shared some further thoughts about the biblical metaphor with me.

Choice Clay

'I am just like you before God; I too have been taken from clay' (Job 33:6).

The cups holding the hot drinks most of us will sip today – perhaps even while reading *Words of Life* – will have come from clay. Whether made of porcelain, stoneware or other ceramic, most hot-drink cups started as some form of clay.

The art of the potter dates back millennia. The most ancient fired objects have been found in today's Czech Republic, southern China, Japan, northern Africa and South America. It is thought that the earliest 'firing' of clay was done in bonfires.

Later people dug trench kilns in the ground and piled the fuel on top for a more controlled firing. To restrain shrinkage and allow moisture to escape, the earliest materials had to be tempered with coarse particles. To avoid angles which were susceptible to cracking, objects were generally curved, even at the bottom.

Artisans discovered that, long before the forming or the firing, the task all started with the selection of the clay. A successful end product initially depended on materials chosen. So a potter had to have an eye for perfection and beauty even in the raw clay. Today commercially prepared clay is available, but potters in Bible times quarried their own material. They dug deep for a good vein and judged the quality of what they found by sight and touch. They saw potential in it and knew what it would take to give it needed pliability and flexibility.

We offer the clay of our lives to the divine potter's hands and with songwriter Jessie Mountain in the song, 'Into Thy Hands, Lord', we pray:

> Not in my own strength can I accomplish
> All thou art planning for me, day by day;
> Owning the limit of human endeavour,
> Humbly I seek, Lord, the grace to obey.
> (*SASB* 501)

Worked and Rested

'*The* LORD *will fight for you; you need only to be still*' (*Exodus 14:14*).

Years ago my husband and I tried our hand at making a few useful ceramic gifts for family. We didn't form clay into objects, but chose green ware made from slip which had been poured in moulds. We trimmed the seams and painted the objects with glaze.

The slip started as clay. Raw clay may hold natural foreign fragments. Once they're picked out, water is added to make the clay into slip. The slip goes through a sieve to strain out even tinier bits. Before the eighteenth century, when the potter's wheel was still the most effective way of producing pieces, what remained of the strained slip was dried to a practical consistency. Then either manually or mechanically, the clay was worked to remove the air and ensure consistent moisture content throughout.

A potter explains that when the prophet–observer says, 'But the pot he was shaping from the clay was marred in his hands; so the potter formed it into another' (Jeremiah 18:4), it signifies that the clay was not prepared properly.

Some clay is too chalky, too friable, too heavy, too dull, too dry, too peppered with extraneous matter, too inflexible, too plastic, too hard, too soft. Some of these problems can be remedied. For example, 'grog' made from broken, pulverised pieces of fired pottery can be added to plastic clay to strengthen it.

The clay needs to be worked to remove air pockets. Sometimes it is trodden on (Isaiah 41:25), slammed on a hard surface, cut, or kneaded like bread. The master knows when the clay is of the right consistency for use and then rests the clay to improve its pliability.

Rest is a stabiliser that gives balance to life. God created the first human being from the dust of the ground. Humankind, the acme of God's creation, appeared on the sixth day (Genesis 1:26, 27, 31). The next day, their first full day, was a day of rest. The divine potter knows when and how to work circumstances of our lives to bring us to an optimum serviceable condition for his use. Do we trust him and rest in him?

Q – Qoph

*'Hear me, as thy love is unchanging, and give me life, O LORD,
by thy decree' (v. 149, NEB).*

On almost any topic, the internet offers a plethora of fact and opinion, news and trivia. We are captivated, one click at a time. Since it is available 24/7, it draws followers at all hours – even if rising before the rest of the household or awake in the night. Some films portray characters trying to catch up by furtively checking e-mails while their neighbours sleep.

In today's segment of Psalm 119 the writer tells of being up before dawn and in the night, but not to search the internet or stay ahead of tyrannical e-mail, but to call out to God and think about his words. He prays with his whole heart and promises to do what God directs (v. 145). The writer is deeply troubled and wants help, assurance and answers. Answer me, save me, hear my voice, preserve my life, he pleads. We all know such times.

It may seem easy to steer a boat on clear days, in calm, well-known waters. We avoid obvious obstacles and stay alert for signs of submerged rocks or shifting sandbars. But when storms limit visibility and churn the waters, we know we can't navigate safely. That's when we're glad to trust an experienced captain who knows the waters and follows proven charts.

In today's portion of the psalm, the writer maintains the reliability of God's faithful love, his nearness, the truth of his commands and their enduring quality. These are our hope too. Relying on them rather than our own limited understanding is vital and never more so than when it's difficult to see clearly in life's turbulence.

The writer of Proverbs puts it another way: 'Trust GOD from the bottom of your heart; don't try to figure out everything on your own. Listen for GOD's voice in everything you do, everywhere you go; he's the one who will keep you on track' (Proverbs 3:5, 6, *MSG*).

Dialogue

'Yet, O LORD, you are our Father. We are the clay, you are the potter;
we are all the work of your hand' (v. 8).

Near the close of the book of Isaiah, after the passages about the Messiah and the coming restoration, chapters 64 to 66 contain a dialogue between God and his people. The prophet recalls God's powerful intervention for them in the past when they followed God's ways and waited for him. Isaiah admits that their bleak state stems from their collective and individual moral failures and prays that God will turn to them as they return to him. Our key verse in which Isaiah refers to us as clay is in that context.

Some say that during the preparation process of working the clay there is an unspoken dialogue which develops between potter and clay. If the preparation process of working the clay seems monotonous to a potter who may identify with the stubborn clay, imagine how the Master Potter feels. He could instantly transform us, his clay, but to do so would impede our development. So he chooses to use the kneading, slicing, slamming aspects of life to help us mature. It's the clay that needs the workout, not the potter.

Major Keith Wallis, a trained potter, observed an exhibit of hand-built Korean pots that communicated the hand, eye and mind of the potter who made them. He noted the great freedom of expression and apparent dialogue between master and material which indicated the potter's enjoyment of the clay for its own qualities and its responsiveness to his touch and said: 'If the pots had turned out differently he would have made something of them because he knew what he was doing and loved his material anyway.'

The Lord names and invites us, the work of his hands, into loving dialogue with him chiefly through worship, his word and prayer. During the Last Supper Jesus faces the reality of betrayal and denial and then offers the disciples comfort and encouragement. He promises to send the Holy Spirit and reminds them: 'You didn't choose me. I chose you' (John 15:16). He then prays for them and for us. Part of the beauty of potter and clay is in the dialogue.

Holy and Whole

'May God himself, the God who makes everything holy and whole, make you holy and whole, put you together – spirit, soul, and body – and keep you fit for the coming of our Master, Jesus Christ' (v. 23, MSG).

God shapes us to his design through a balance of our inner God-given aspirations, desires, needs, inclinations and abilities as well as our outer circumstances, situations and opportunities.

We can choose the way of the wheel (the cross); choose to remain pliable and responsive. The potter's firm but gentle touch is a balance of inside and out, space and contour, swelling and constriction, requiring both of his hands (of freedom and discipline). If we determine to trust God, are willing for him to place us on his wheel, give ourselves to him and relax in his hands, we can count on his Spirit's loving imprint on our lives.

In his book about holiness, *Never the Same Again*, General Shaw Clifton writes:

> I like what Bramwell Tripp wrote once. He summed up the possibility of pragmatic holiness in three pithy sentences: 1. To say 'I must sin' is to deny my Saviour. 2. To say 'I cannot sin' is to deceive myself. 3. To say 'I need not sin' is to declare my faith in divine power![7]

Believing that third possibility, we confidently pray with songwriter Darlene Zschech:

> Take me, mould me, use me, fill me
> I give my life to the Potter's hand
> Call me, guide me, lead me, walk
>   beside me
> I give my life to the Potter's hand.[8]

———————

To ponder:

At age twenty-three, early day Salvationist Mildred Duff said: 'My chief reason for throwing in my lot with The Salvation Army was its faith and teaching that God can keep those who trust him wholly pure and blameless.'[9]

On the Wheel

*'That's why we can be so sure that every detail in our lives of love
for God is worked into something good' (v. 28, MSG).*

Working with clay in free form allows freedom to change during the process, but potters creating on wheels have to decide the types of objects they plan to make and form the vessels accordingly. In a process called 'throwing' (from an Old English word, *thrawan*, meaning to twist or turn), the potter firmly holds a ball of clay in the centre of the turntable or wheel-head, and then rotates the wheel by hand, by foot pedal or by electric motor.

The potter can proceed only when the clay is perfectly centred. The motion of the wheel is repetitive. Through continual turning, the clay can rise to become a smooth and balanced vessel under the potter's hand.

God prepares us through what sometimes seems like repetitious routine. He stretches us and corrects us while respecting our unique differences. Whatever changes the potter makes, he makes while his pot is in motion since that's when it's the most responsive. If we have yielded our lives to God and have been set in motion on his wheel, we are more receptive to his direction. If he apprises us of something, we can respond without delay, knowing he'll take care of whatever comes next.

Circumstances can be God's potter's wheel for us. *Circum* means around and stance comes from *stare*, meaning to stand. Our situation may not seem important, but if we are faithful in it the Lord will use our circle of routine to strengthen us and make us pleasing to him.

Sometimes pottery needs to be reshaped a little or a lot. Perhaps the clay on the wheel is off centre. The vessel starts to rise a few inches, the potter sees a flaw and, rather than take a chance, thumps it down to start again. Or further on in the process, the shape is out of kilter, wobbles, needs correction. Fortunately, clay can be recycled and reworked. If necessary, we can be too. Our transformation requires our repentance and God's grace of restoration.

Glaze and Fire

*'Now faith is being sure of what we hope for and certain of
what we do not see' (v. 1).*

After waiting for the clay to thoroughly dry, the potter usually paints the
object with an opaque watery glaze. The heat of the kiln hardens
the glaze, reveals its pigment and makes it inseparable from the pottery.

In her book, *Worthy Vessels*, Nell Kennedy tells of the founder of
Doshisha University in Japan. Niijima Jo (or Joseph Hardy Neeshima,
as he came to be called) was united to Christ and experienced the fire of
opposition and hardship, yet remained inseparable from his Lord.

Niijima Jo was born in 1843, the son of a samurai-class family. During
his youth, he discovered a friend's Chinese Bible. Although at that time
the Bible was forbidden in Japan, he read it in secret and was so impressed
by what it said that he dared to seek surreptitious passage to America to
learn more about God. In Shanghai he sold his swords to buy a New
Testament and endured hardships to learn English. He wanted others to
know Christ too.

When Neeshima arrived in Massachusetts, Alpheus Hardy, the owner of
the ship on which he'd sailed, arranged for his education. Neeshima
publicly professed his faith in 1866. After college he attended seminary,
where he was ordained. With funds from American churches, he returned
to Japan in 1875 to found a Christian school in Japan's cultural capital,
Kyoto.

Although Neeshima, a nineteenth-century hero of faith, died at the age
of forty-six, his transformed life and commitment to the gospel continued
to influence many Doshisha students. Before The Salvation Army arrived
in Japan, Gunpei Yamamuro, who would become the first Japanese
Salvation Army officer, studied at Doshisha. The government named
Yamamuro as one of the greatest social workers in Japanese history.
Salvationists consider him the father of the Army in Japan.

The fires of hardship and sacrifice served only to strengthen the
courage and vision of these heroes who abandoned themselves to God and
his purposes.

Broken Pieces

*'Woe to him . . . who is but a potsherd among the potsherds
on the ground' (Isaiah 45:9).*

The 'Field of Blood' (v. 8) wasn't always a burial ground. The priests purchased the plot with the coins Judas remorsefully returned. Since they didn't want anything to do with 'blood money' and couldn't legally put it into the temple treasury, they bought a field to bury foreigners who died in Jerusalem. The transaction remains a monument to their treachery and to the innocence of Christ. It also fulfilled Old Testament prophecy (see Zechariah 11:12, 13).

The field had been a potter's field. If it was a place where potters dug clay through the years, then it wouldn't be useful tillable land and would be cheap to buy. Whether in this same area or another one outside of Jerusalem, potters and others disposed of broken pottery as into a landfill. God directed Jeremiah to such an area – the Potsherd Gate – to deliver a message through an object lesson of broken vessels (Jeremiah 19:1–3).

Discarded hard, broken pieces are generally a metaphor for dryness, uselessness, judgment or death (see Psalm 22:15, Jeremiah 22:28, Isaiah 30:14, Job 2:8, Jeremiah 19:10, 11, Revelation 22:27 and Psalm 31:12). Since shards are not biodegradable, archaeologists have used them to uncover history.

But broken, discarded pottery can be recycled. As we noted on Saturday, pulverised shards can be worked into new batches of clay to strengthen them. Even pottery glaze contains some ground shards. Sin shatters. Our sin crushed the Saviour, but he conquered death. If we come to the Risen Lord in penitence, he forgives and transforms us. We can pray with hymnwriter Leslie Taylor-Hunt:

> Master, I yield to thee,
> Crumble, then fashion me
> Flawless, and fit to be
> Indwelt by thee.
>   (*SASB* 416)

Everyday Vessels

'Does not the potter have the right to make out of the same lump of clay some pottery for noble purposes and some for common use?' (Romans 9:21).

It's amazing to consider the numerous useful things in which some form of clay is used: bricks and bowls, surgical tools and implants, electronic devices, insulators, spark plugs, orthopaedic joint replacements, dentures, microwave ovens, televisions, ceramic heaters, catalytic converters, space-shuttle heat shields and more.

Setting technological uses aside, potters of the past would be amazed even at today's variety of household items. Potters in biblical times chiefly made everyday pieces. In both Old and New Testaments we read of earthenware pots, jugs, pitchers, jars, bowls, dishes, cups and lamps. Sometimes Scripture uses pottery as an object lesson, but we also recall accounts in which Elijah, Elisha, Gideon and Jesus used actual pottery.

In the tabernacle or temple, objects sometimes similar to everyday pieces were chiefly made of gold or bronze and more highly esteemed. In Lamentations 4 the prophet contrasts the deplorable state of the nation with what they once had been when they followed the Lord. He says they were once worth their weight in gold, but are now regarded as only clay pots.

Although there were stone containers as well as some wooden pitchers or bowls in everyday use, since clay was cheap and readily available, most of the ordinary person's vessels, cookware and crockery were pottery.

Pottery can be an apt metaphor for the common person. As we saw earlier, Scripture also refers to God as our potter. In today's passage the Lord tells Jeremiah that he'll give him a message at the potter's house. God's use of the metaphor of potter and clay, and choice of the pottery shed in which to deliver his divine message, also seem to show respect for the worker in clay and dignify what he makes, however commonplace. We can confidently commit ourselves, ordinary as we may be, to our heavenly potter's hands.

R – *Resh*

*'Defend my cause and redeem me; preserve my life
according to your promise' (v. 154).*

In this section, a concept from our key verse stands out. One translator
suggests using 'fight my fight' for 'defend my cause' as in the way David
pleads in Psalm 35:1: 'Contend, O LORD, with those who contend with me;
fight against those who fight against me.' The *New English Bible* states the
key verse: 'Be thou my advocate and win release for me; true to thy
promise, give me life.'

The root of the word advocate means 'one called to one's aid'. From the
German word for advocate, *fürspreche*, we infer 'speaking for another'.
The Greek word used for the Holy Spirit in the New Testament,
Parakletos, also springs to mind. Jews sometimes transliterated that word
into Hebrew letters and used it to mean the defence one's good deeds and
obedience accrued before God.

But our Christian defence is not our accumulated righteousness, but the
advocacy of Christ who saved us and intercedes for us. As John writes in
his Epistle: 'My little children, these things I write to you, so that you may
not sin. And if anyone sins, we have an Advocate with the Father, Jesus
Christ the righteous' (1 John 2:1, *NKJV*). The word advocate here is the
same term used elsewhere in the New Testament for the Holy Spirit.
Christ's work for us is inseparable from his Spirit's working in us.

One of our sons is a military lawyer. He thoroughly prepares each case
according to military law provided in the Uniform Code of Military
Justice. In verse 160 the psalmist aptly reminds us that what God says is
the vital and ageless basis of his dealings with people. In light of our need
and God's provision we humbly pray with Salvation Army songwriter
Albert Orsborn:

Only thou art still my soul's defender,
Hand of strength, and all-prevenient grace;
Frail am I, but thou art my befriender,
And I trust the shining of thy face.

(*SASB* 762)

His Worthy Vessels

'He will rejoice over you with singing' (Zephaniah 3:17).

Potters open their kilns with great expectation, even when they primarily contain such ordinary, useful objects as jars, jugs, bowls, pitchers, lamps, cups, dishes, basins.

During a drought, when Elijah asked a widow for something to eat she complied, even though she had planned to use the last of her nearly empty *jar* of flour and *jug* of oil for a final meal before dying. The prophet assured her that the Lord would keep her jar and jug supplied throughout the drought. Miraculously he did (1 Kings 17).

Elijah ordered that twelve *jarfuls* of water be poured on the offering on Carmel so that there would be no question when the Lord answered prayer with fire (1 Kings 18).

A prophet's widow appealed to Elisha for help in her poverty. He advised her to borrow many *jars* and start pouring what oil she had into them. The oil flowed until every one was full. She sold the oil to pay debts and still had income to live on (2 Kings 4).

Gideon's band of 300 concealed their torches in *pitchers* until the signal was given to smash them and shout for victory (Judges 7).

When Jesus encounters the woman at Jacob's well, she interrupts her clandestine errand, leaves her water *jar* and openly spreads the news of the Messiah to her town (John 4). On Maundy Thursday Jesus sends two disciples ahead to prepare for the Passover meal and tells them they'll meet a man carrying an *earthen jug* of water. It may be easier to notice a man who is doing what was generally a woman's task.

That *jug* may have supplied the *pitcher and wash basin* Jesus used to wash the disciples' feet during the Last Supper. We also recall Jesus' reference to the *dish and the cup* that night. John even mentions a *jar* of vinegar at the cross (John 19:29).

The potter celebrates every piece he takes from the kiln. When yielded to and refined by God, we are transformed from clay to useful objects, meant to be filled, poured out and filled again. In his eyes and for his use, we are his worthy vessels. We follow Paul's lead in Colossians 1 and pray for each other that we may live lives worthy of the Lord and pleasing to him (vv. 9, 10).

Everyday Holiness

By guest writer Major Anita M. Caldwell (Tbilisi, Georgia)

Introduction

While growing up in the little town of Eldred, Pennsylvania, USA, I had the privilege of hearing my father preach holiness nearly every Sunday. He seldom strayed from the call for holy living. At age fifteen, I rededicated my life to Christ. Over the next two years, the Holy Spirit was gracious to show me how selfish I really was. At age eighteen, while I knelt at a camp-meeting altar, God sanctified my soul. His Spirit has guided me to do his will. He has led me to serve him in the USA, Haiti, Moldova, Russia and Georgia, also to minister in Romania and Ukraine.

During this series we will look at holiness truths, holiness myths and holiness exercises. My special thanks go to my husband Brad for being the initial editor of these writings.

Holiness truths

In our world today there is one great question – what is truth? When considering holiness, we want to know what the truth is. Can we live holy lives? Could such a life be possible for me? The answer is yes! Holy living is possible. And holy living is essential.

Holiness myths

Throughout my life I have discovered several myths about the doctrine of holiness. Some educators either avoid the doctrine completely or try to make it something achievable outside God's terms. As an education leader in Eastern Europe, I have learned that open and honest discussion is the best teaching method for this tenet of faith. In such moments together we discover our fears and our hopes for a holy heart.

Holiness exercises

We understand the importance of physical exercise but do we consider the need to make holiness a part of our daily spiritual life? In the third set of these devotions we will consider exercises to help us keep fit spiritually.

Let's be passionate about holy living! Our lives will be blessed.

Holiness – God's Choice for Us

'He chose us in him before the foundation of the world, that we should be holy and without blame before him in love' (v. 4, NKJV).

Of the billions of people in the world, God chose to create you! You are a unique creation. There is not one other person with your exact nose, eyes, facial expressions. You were chosen to be born into this world and God has a special purpose for your life.

Before creation, God determined that we should be holy. Holy living is not a new concept – it has been God's choice for us from the foundation of the world. He calls us to be a holy people. But being holy is a tall order. We want to be like Christ in our day-to-day living. We want to live honestly. We try to be kind to our neighbour who tosses his rubbish into our yard every day. However, we find this humanly impossible to accomplish.

In Eastern Europe, the word 'holy' specifically describes the saint who has been anointed by the Orthodox Church and placed on an icon. Hence, to be 'holy' is completely impossible to consider. Monks in the monasteries are holy. The priest is holy. But common people cannot be holy, by the very definition of the word.

Come with me on a journey for the next four weeks. Let's discover together what God has to say about holy living. Is it possible? The Salvation Army's founder, William Booth, believed it was when he said,

Come along, my comrades. Your happiness and your influence are all connected with your being made holy. Oh, I beseech you to kneel down here and now, and ask God to make you each and all pure, by the power of the Holy Ghost, through the blood of the Lamb.[10]

———

To pray:

Lord, I cannot be holy in my own strength! Give me the power to live above sin each day. I will listen to you; I will submit to your voice, I choose to obey you. Amen.

Holiness – A Call to a Life without Sin

*'May he strengthen your hearts so that you will be blameless and
holy in the presence of our God and Father when our Lord
Jesus Christ comes with all his holy ones' (v. 13).*

Our Moscow women's group agreed to meet once a week to study holy
living. Our first meeting was an open discussion about God calling us
to live holy lives. One woman spoke up: 'I know God says we must be holy
but he does not really mean we can be holy. He knows we can't. It is not
possible!' Each week, we continued to study God's word together. We
discussed living above sin at great length. Finally one of the ladies dropped
her eyes to her Bible and said, 'Not only does God ask us to be holy but I
guess it is true – we can be holy. We can live without sin.'

Around the world today there are hosts of people who believe we are
sinning Christians. This disease has crept into every denomination and
church. The belief is that in our humanity we have no choice but to sin. It
overtakes us and we sin without choice.

The question lies in the definition of the word sin. In Wesley's definition,
it is rebellion against a known law of God. God holds us accountable for
what we know is wrong. Lying, cheating, stealing and all other violations of
God's clear commandments are sins of choice. If we are about to lie, we
know it and we have the choice to choose to tell the truth. If we are thinking
about stealing, we know this and we have the choice to walk away.

I remember having this choice as a child. I stood in our town's Five and
Ten store considering a ring my mother would not let me have. I remember
reaching out to take it and stepping back. Finally, I walked away – and what
a relief flooded my soul!

Walk away from sin! This is a life of victory over sin. Be excited about a
life free from guilt. The Holy Spirit can and will alert you; the Holy Spirit
can and will empower you to not choose sin; the Holy Spirit will give you
an amazing peace that comes with a guilt-free life. You can do it by his
grace and strength.

Holiness – God's Will for Us

'For this is the will of God: your sanctification' (v. 3, NKJV).

It was another beautiful day in Haiti. As a nurse I was responsible for distributing vitamins and medications to our clinic patients. I had just finished helping a young mother with her baby, and in my best Creole I told her she could go. She went to the door and just stood there. Thinking that perhaps she did not understand my Creole, I asked a longer-term missionary to tell her she was free to go.

This time, she readjusted her baby, gave a sigh but continued to stand before the closed door. Suddenly, we realised that she did not know how to turn the door knob and open the door. Her home had no such door knobs, only a lean-to grass door. I went and turned the door knob, and she left with the medication she needed for her child.

God has provided a way for us to walk through the door of holiness and step into a new life of faith in him. This is his will for us – it should not be a step we fear or feel impossible. As a Father who loves his children, he would not bring us to this place in our spiritual growth only to force upon us a bitter, unhappy life. He wishes us a grand oasis of spiritual growth.

Salvation and forgiveness from our past sins is wonderful. Knowing that guilt is lifted from our hearts and minds is freedom. Salvation is the first step of holy living – initial sanctification. However, entire sanctification is a place of full freedom in Christ – it is the sometimes disparaged door to heart purity.

We come to a place in our spiritual growth where we willingly submit our selfish desires to the will of God. This decision to allow him full control of our lives invites him to fully equip us to obey him. We are entirely empowered to serve him, to obey him, to heed his calling.

To pray:

Lord, help me to trust you to open the door to holy living, even while I am not yet sure how to turn the knob.

Holiness – God's Command

'Be holy, for I am holy' (v. 16, NKJV).

At age four, my son Justin wanted nothing more than to discover what the roots of plants looked like. It did not matter that the plants could be damaged by being uprooted. It did not matter that he would be punished for his actions. It did not matter how many times he was told to stop. He just kept pulling the plants out of their dirt.

Only escalation of punishment convinced him that he should alter his behaviour. His penalty advanced from a talk with me, his mother, to increasingly serious punishments, until he decided he really did not want to deal with the punishment any longer. He changed his circumstances by ceasing to uproot my plants.

God does not compel us so directly to obey him. God's commands are not optional, but because we perceive no immediate punishment, we imagine that we can afford a little sin in our lives now and then. We don't really want to hear a particular command and we don't really think it is possible to obey. Yet God's command cannot be ignored. If he calls us, will he not also empower us? We can only agree that he would not command us to do something impossible.

His gift to us is freedom from the guilt of our sin and the power to live above new sin. He longs to bring us to a place of spiritual freedom. This is not a life of drudgery, a life of dos and don'ts, but a life of 'Yes, Lord!' When we come to that place of final submission to him – without his compulsion – obedience is a spiritual joy. Our will is to do his will.

God commands us to be holy. We can't be, but he can enable us, if we allow him complete control of our lives without waiting for divine punishment to drive us there.

To ponder:

'Holiness does not begin with an outward conformity of habit but with an inward receiving of the Spirit.'

Frederick Coutts[11]

Holiness – Provided by Jesus' Atonement

*'And so Jesus also suffered outside the city gate to make the
people holy through his own blood' (v. 12).*

The worship meeting had been very special and the sermon concerned
holy living. Many people knelt at the altar to pray and I had chosen to
kneel beside Desann. It was one of the normal hot Sundays in Haiti, but as
we knelt together on the cement floor at the wooden altar, we did not really
take note of the heat.

God was at work in the hearts of a multitude of people, especially
Desann's. He appeared to be a young child of ten when indeed he was a
young man closer to sixteen. In Haiti the children do not get enough
protein or food in general, and therefore their growth is much slower.

His prayer was very earnest, and finally we stood knowing that he had
taken a new step of faith. Through a translator, I asked him about his
prayer time. He responded, 'I asked the Lord to take my pride!' I could not
imagine how this young boy could have pride in his life. I later discovered
that his father was a witchdoctor and his home was made of blocks and
brightly painted. Desann realised the trap of selfishness and pride. He
knew that day that God had freed him from these spiritual hindrances.

We tend to focus on the fact that Jesus died on the cross to forgive us of
our past sins. We don't often consider the fact that through his death and
resurrection, we can experience a holy future. We believe he can save us
from our sins but we doubt that he can save us from ourselves.

Jesus died on the cross to forgive our sinful actions and to free us from
our sinful selfishness. When we submit to his will, he takes our life, our will
and our self, cleanses it from all unrighteousness and empowers us to live
above sin.

To pray:

Lord, help me know you can make me holy and keep me holy. Amen.

S – *Shin*

'Great peace have they who love your law, and nothing can make them stumble' (v. 165).

A decorative blue-and-white plate from Israel with the word *shalom* painted in Hebrew hangs on our wall. The first letter in shalom ('s' or *shin*) is the letter featured in today's section of Psalm 119 – the one which begins each verse: *sarim* (princes), *sas* (rejoice), *sheqer* (lying), *sheba* (seven times), *shalom* (peace) *sibbarti* (I have hoped), *shamrah* (they have kept) and *shamarti* (I have kept).

We remember that in this acrostic psalm the writer begins each of the eight verses in a section with a particular letter of the Hebrew alphabet.

In spite of ongoing persecution, rather than in awe of the enemy, the psalmist stands in awe of God's word. He knows the joy of discovering treasure as he continues to hold onto God's promise. Love for God's word helps him discern and prefer truth.

His heart is full of praise and he frequently expresses it. In verse 164 he says he praises God seven times a day. This could mean perpetually or it could mean at seven specified times. The Jews praised God twice before the morning reading of the Decalogue, once afterwards, twice before the evening reading and twice afterwards – seven specified times.

In a different setting, in Sunday sermons during Lent in the late tenth century, Christians were asked to remember Christ and his cross at daybreak, 9 a.m., midday, 3 p.m., evening, bedtime and, if they woke, in the middle of the night – seven specified times.

Then comes what seems to be the crux of our portion of Psalm 119, our key verse: because the psalmist loves God's word, he experiences profound peace, even in the midst of trouble. While established in the word, no obstacle can cause him to stumble. Practising obedience to what he knows of God's will, he looks for God's deliverance and lives his life as an open book before the Lord – and we can too.

Holiness – Baptism of the Holy Spirit

'I baptise you with water for repentance but one who is more powerful than I is coming after me; I am not worthy to carry his sandals. He will baptise you with the Holy Spirit and fire' (v. 11).

William Booth wrote, 'This is the fiery baptism which burns up hatred, and grudges, and self-seeking, and self-will, and purifies all our motives and affections.'[12] This is the baptism we seek. Yes, we must first give ourselves completely to God and he baptises us with the fire of the Holy Ghost and cleanses us.

Growing up on a farm, we loved to go barefoot. At least once a week a splinter would find its way into the bottom of my foot or hand. Mom would take a needle from the sewing kit but before she would use it, she always 'passed it through the fire' on the gas stove. I now realise that she was purifying the needle with the fire so it could cause no infection. She would carefully remove the sliver of wood and then cleanse the wound with peroxide. It was not a fun process but it worked!

Similarly, the baptism of the Holy Ghost is not an emotional high or a special gift but a true inward cleansing, a true inward purifying of the soul. No, not a magical change, but 'burning away' proud selfishness and leaving only humble willingness and submission to the daily leading of the Holy Spirit. It is not often an easy choice for us because we want our own way. We want our will. If we will but trust our God, he will baptise us 'with the Holy Spirit and fire'.

Again from William Booth: 'God is waiting to cleanse you. What doth hinder your receiving the purifying baptism? "Now is the accepted time." Tell God that all the doubtful things shall be given up, and then go down before him.'[13]

To pray:

Dear Lord, show me how to believe. Help me to believe that you can cleanse and make me holy. Amen.

Holiness – Lived Today . . .
Rewarded Tomorrow

'Make every effort to live in peace with all men and to be holy;
without holiness no-one will see the Lord' (v. 14).

This command is for today and tomorrow. 'Be holy' is a present-day requirement. Many hope that in death they will be holy. Some hope that over the years they can become holy. Today is the day to be holy. Tomorrow, the reward is that we will see the Lord. We understand that God is holy. We believe we know a few people in our lives that might be holy.

But our honest question is how can I be holy? We realise that God commands holiness and we agree that we should be holy but the writer of Hebrews hits the nail on the head by connecting holiness and living at peace with all people. If we could live alone on a mountain top, the possibility of holy living seems much greater.

Living here on earth with the hurt and pain that people inject into our lives seems to make holiness completely impossible. And it is impossible if we attempt peace with all people in our own strength.

The Holy Spirit was sent to be our Comforter and our Teacher. He was sent to give us power, and that power is power over sin. He alerts us and makes a way of escape from sin. He is the one who calls us to be kind to those around us. He is the one who whispers to our hearts when we are not making the effort to live in peace with all people. He is the one who guides us to a change in our thoughts towards others. He is the one who nudges us to humble ourselves when it seems impossible.

The Holy Spirit is our great Gift, our Teacher who guides us into all truth. The one requirement is that we live close enough to him that we can hear his voice and obey him.

There is a lie whispered to each of our hearts that this is not possible. Yet, we know that with God all things are possible. By living a holy life today, we have a promise of seeing the Lord tomorrow!

Holiness – Promised to All Who Believe

'May God himself, the God of peace, sanctify you through and through. May your whole spirit, soul and body be kept blameless at the coming of our Lord Jesus Christ. The one who calls you is faithful and he will do it' (vv. 23, 24).

We take care when we walk along the icy streets of Moscow in the winter. Two to three inches of ice await those who walk on it with disregard. However, the path less used is much safer, for the snow has not yet been packed and become slippery ice. Holiness is the path less trod but it is the safe path to heaven.

Verse 23 is incorporated in The Salvation Army's tenth doctrine: 'We believe that it is the privilege of all believers to be wholly sanctified, and that their whole spirit and soul and body may be preserved blameless unto the coming of our Lord Jesus Christ.'

Early day Salvationist preacher Samuel Logan Brengle wrote a very clear outline of what we need to prepare our hearts for the work of the Holy Spirit:

1. We must be rid of sin.
2. We must be at peace with our fellow men and women.
3. We must consent for the Holy Spirit to have his way with us.
4. We must have faith that God will grant us his Spirit, and that he is more willing to give than we are to receive.

Verse 24 is the promise that the same God who calls us to holiness will enable us to live holy lives. So we need not doubt him!

We are such a privileged people to know such a Holy Spirit! He has not come to hurt us or to make our life miserable. The precious Holy Spirit has come to anoint us for ministry. He comes to teach us all things. He comes to guide us into all truth. He is on our side, cheering for us, encouraging us, empowering us to reach the prize.

To pray:

Precious Holy Spirit, I ask you just now to come into my life. I am ready to obey your voice. I am ready to obey your calling to be holy. Guide me into all truth! Fill me with your power to overcome sin. Comfort me in times of despair. Teach me to walk in your ways. Amen.

Myth 1 – Holiness is a Set of Rules

'For the LORD does not see as man sees; for man looks at the outward appearance, but the LORD looks at the heart' (v. 7, NKJV).

We know this story well. Samuel was looking for God's choice while others judged who should be anointed according to size. Samuel had told David's family to sanctify themselves – to set themselves apart. Still they looked at the outward appearance when God was looking at David's heart.

God wants to anoint men and women for his service, but holiness is not a set of rules that requires a certain outward appearance. My parents were both preachers and teachers of holiness. However, woven into their doctrine was the idea that outward dress was a witness of a holy lifestyle. I soon discovered that dressing according to their expectations did not change my heart. I also discovered that there were many religious people professing holiness who were extremely critical and judgmental.

There are too many people who have perfected their outward appearance but inside are empty of joy, empty of peace, and empty of hope. We may wear the Salvation Army uniform, but it does not make us holy. We may attend church every Sunday, but it does not make us holy. Only the Holy Spirit can guide us to his holiness, and when he does we find that we are changed within our very souls.

The outcome of a changed heart is that we joyfully obey God's Word. We no longer view it as law but grace. It is no longer a hardship but a pleasure. What were once rules become our goals.

Sets of rules make holy living appear to be a life of drudgery without joy. The holy life should be the exact opposite! We can be excited about this life empowered by the Holy Spirit. It is a life filled with exhilarating days for the Lord, filled with his blessings through the power of the Holy Spirit.

Human beings look on the outside, but God looks at the heart. He has changed us from the inside out. We are blessed by his ability to make us holy and keep us holy.

Myth 2 – Holiness is about Tradition

*'He said to them, "All too well you reject the commandment of God,
that you may keep your tradition"' (v. 9, NKJV).*

Traditions can be wonderful. Each of us has special Christmas and
Easter traditions. We have developed worship traditions as well. In
some worship environments we want to stand while we sing and sit while
we pray. For others, we like to sit while we sing and stand while we pray.
In Russia there are no seats in the state church so everyone stands when
attending a worship service.

I grew up in a holiness denomination where we knelt when we prayed.
Likewise, we carefully chose holiness songs to sing as well as songs about
the blood of Christ shed for our sins. Tradition dictated the service format,
and sacred dance could never have been included because it would not
have been thought 'holy'.

In The Salvation Army, we call our Sunday morning meeting the holiness meeting. Many of our places of worship have holiness tables inscribed
with the words 'Holiness unto the Lord'. One of the colours of our flag –
blue – represents the holiness of God. The simple cross that is often found
in our halls and chapels reminds us to live like Christ. Each of these is a
meaningful tradition of faith.

While tradition is not wrong, holiness is not about tradition. We have
wonderful holiness songs in the old hymns of the Church, and we have
clear holiness songs in today's praise and worship. We can bow our heads
at the mercy seat or holiness table, and yet walk away unholy. True worship
comes from the heart. In our Scripture reading today, Jesus had harsh
words about mishandling tradition.

True holiness is about a changed life and choosing a sin-free life. While
tradition can encourage holiness, it cannot cleanse our hearts. Tradition
may call us to holy living, but each Christian must choose to obey God
daily.

To ponder:

**Do I base my holiness on traditions or have I allowed Christ to change me within
and to renew that change daily?**

45

Myth 3 – Holiness is for the Saint

'To the church of God which is at Corinth, to those who are sanctified in Christ Jesus, called to be saints, with all who in every place call on the name of Jesus Christ our Lord, both theirs and ours' (v. 2, NKJV).

Sometimes we imagine that holiness is reserved for elderly believers. We sense they are preparing for another life. They consistently pray and read their Bibles. Faith seems to be easier for them. We reserve the title of saint for them. We tend to believe that one day we too will reach an age that allows us to have a holy life.

At other times, holiness seems to belong to the monk. In Moldova, I visited a monk who lives in an ancient monastery built in the side of a cliff. Seeing by candlelight and sleeping on a rock floor, he says little, but the life he has chosen speaks volumes. Few in the world today can choose such a simple life dedicated to the worship of God alone.

Some believe a holy person is the person sainted by the Church. This is very true in minds of those who live in Eastern Europe. 'Holy' is reserved for the person whose face is already on the holy icon and holiness seems completely impossible for anyone living today.

In each case, these people are just normal people who set their lives aside to be led by the Holy Spirit. No matter their age, their dedication, their place in history, each of them has had temptations; each has had to choose Christ each day.

In our Scripture reading, Paul says we are *all* called to the holy life of a saint. This call is for people of all ages and circumstances. Holiness is available for all who are willing to entrust their lives to God. Holy living is a daily choice – impossible in our own strength but possible through the power of the Holy Spirit.

———

To pray:

Lord, cleanse my heart and renew a right spirit within me today. Fill me with your Holy Spirit. Help me hear your voice and obey you in each decision I make today. Make me strong to withstand the temptations I will face. Amen.

T – *Tau*

'Invigorate my soul so I can praise you well, use your decrees to put iron in my soul' (v. 175, MSG).

The final segment of Psalm 119 can be a prayer, especially if we read it in *The Message* or the *New Living Translation*. The psalmist starts by personifying his cry and his supplication. In verses 169 and 170, he describes his prayers as messengers who on his behalf go before the Lord to seek insight and deliverance.

If we could visualise these messengers, would they look like computer graphics or abstractions? Perhaps they would look like the distressed figure in Munch's painting, *The Scream*. Or they might seem like one of Chagall's floating figures such as *The Blue Violinist*. If we followed the psalmist's lead of personification, what would our own prayers look like?

The writer then says that he wants to freely verbalise his praise to God for teaching him his will and to wholeheartedly sing about the excellence of God's word, its rightness and righteousness.

Then when the psalmist says he's chosen God's precepts (v. 173); longs for his salvation; finds delight in divine law (v. 174); seeks life and sustenance from God and his word (v. 175), why in the closing moments of the psalm does he describe himself as a lost sheep? Commentator A. F. Kirkpatrick helpfully suggests:

> The psalmist is describing his outward circumstances rather than his spiritual state, the helplessness of his condition rather than his moral failures . . . Like a sheep that has been separated from the flock he is exposed to constant dangers, and therefore he beseeches God not to leave him to wander alone, but in accordance with his promise (Ezekiel 34:11 ff) to seek for him, for amid all these dangers he does not forget God's law.[14]

If we choose to saturate ourselves in God's word, we too will recognise the Shepherd's voice.

Myth 4 – Holiness is a Good Idea
(but it's impossible to be like Christ)

'But the Helper, the Holy Spirit, whom the Father will send in my name, he will teach you all things, and bring to your remembrance all things that I said to you' (v. 26, NKJV).

The easiest definition of holiness is to be Christlike. However, if we honestly think about this for long, we come to the conclusion that it is impossible. Christ died on the cross for the sins of humankind. I cannot do this. Christ let others mock him and spit on him. I find it hard to do this. Once we consider the life of Christ, we come to believe that God has asked us to do something that is impossible.

Let's look a little closer at the life of Christ. In the garden of Gethsemane, we find his friends falling asleep. He wakes them but finally gives up trying to keep them awake to pray. We have experienced the same, and we have loved our friends in spite of their faults. In the temple, Christ became angry with the politics of the day. We have experienced the same and have stated our case. In the wilderness, Christ stood up to the temptations of Satan with the word of God. We have had victory over sin through God's word.

Our great gift is the Spirit of Christ who abides with us and enables us to be like him. He has promised to guide us into all truth (John 16:12). He has promised to convict of sin (John 16:8). He will teach us all things (John 14:26). He has promised to give us power (Acts 1:8). He is our Counsellor (John 14:17). He is our Comforter (John 14:26).

We must realise that he understands our humanness. He created us; he knows us. He acknowledges our weaknesses. He is not waiting with a whip, ready to give us a 'woodshed licking' for our failures. He does expect us to learn from those errors, and to turn from sin – which he enables us to do. He wants us to serve him in obedience to his call.

We can count on him, he will not fail us. He does not call us to something we cannot do. Our task is to obey him. We must believe that if God has called us to be holy, he will also equip us to be holy on this earth. I believe he can and he does. Do you?

Myth 5 – Holiness Can Be Achieved Only in Death

'Therefore, I urge you, brothers, in view of God's mercy, to offer your bodies as living sacrifices, holy and pleasing to God – this is your spiritual act of worship' (v. 1).

A couple of years ago my husband and I stood by the bed of his grandmother as she was dying. She left us with many wonderful memories and a strong encouragement to be faithful to the Lord.

Once you look death in the face you conclude it is a reality you don't want to second guess. We all want to know that there is an eternity of peace and joy waiting for us. We understand that our God is a holy God and that he demands a holy people. We know that heaven will be a holy place and, therefore, if we want to achieve heaven, we must be holy.

The question is: when does holiness occur? Achieving holiness in death would be a great gift and much easier than attempting to be holy on this earth. What if it isn't possible? What if this idea is erroneous? Do we dare take the chance to wait for death to be holy?

In our Scripture reading, being holy is in the present tense. God tells us to 'be holy for I am holy'. This is a command for today. We cannot place our hope in a future death when God has made provision for a holy present and calls us to be holy today.

If we ignore the work of the Holy Spirit in our lives, the outcome of this death myth is that we live a guilt-ridden life, one that is torn between obeying God and yielding to our selfish desires.

Listen to the Holy Spirit's calling, repent of selfish desires and wishes, submit to God's leading in your life, become totally his and then take that step of faith to believe he has sanctified you. We cannot achieve this in death, but solely through the power of the Holy Spirit.

———

To pray:

Lord, sanctify me now, and then give me the desire and courage to live a holy life today.

Myth 6 – Holiness is Impossible
(one cannot live above sin)

'Wash me thoroughly from my iniquity, and cleanse me from my sin'
(v. 2, NKJV).

Each day the internet, television and all other forms of media assault our thinking by normalising sin. It is no wonder that our definition of sin has changed over the years. It is no wonder that what used to be sin is no longer called sin. It is no wonder that we think it is impossible to live above sin. We are desensitised – what once was sin is now the daily norm. Therefore we believe it is not possible to live above sin.

This idea has found its way into hearts around the world. Perhaps it starts with the definition of sin. For me, sin is a wilful transgression against a known law of God. It is not a mistake, not something I have forgotten, but something I choose to do. Even some Christians teach that because we are so fallen, we *cannot* choose to refuse an action as clearly sinful as lying or stealing. Actually, sin is a choice we make. By the power of the Holy Spirit, we can live above *all* sin!

The psalmist knew his sin. He wanted to be cleansed; he wanted a recreated heart.

Perhaps we have lost sight of how great God is! He who created us, who formed the world and holds it in his hand, gives us the power to live above sin. He knows our nature. He created humans and watched as they chose sin in the garden. He gave us the right to choose; he wants us to be free to choose him over sin. He then empowers us to live above sin if we ask him.

To pray:

Lord, I do love you and want to serve you. I do want to live above sin. Please help me to hear your voice above the noise of this world. Help me to understand how much you want to bless me with your power to live above sin. Amen.

Myth 7 – Holiness Perfects Us from Ever Sinning

'My little children, these things I write to you, so that you may not sin.
And if anyone sins, we have an Advocate with the Father,
Jesus Christ the righteous' (v. 1, NKJV).

Holiness is not a magical shield that blocks out sin. We can sin, and mostly likely will, but our sin is not daily or constant. We are not controlled by sin. On the rare occasion that we are caught in temptation and we sin, we readily turn to the Father and plead for forgiveness. The Holy Spirit restores us to a victorious life and we live with clean hearts.

As a young Christian I watched many people around me who actually believed that once they were sanctified it was impossible for them to sin. The outcome of this myth was that when they sinned they would not admit their wrong. They blamed their behaviour on other factors. I did not understand this theology. One thing I did know was that if this was holiness, I wanted no part of it.

Today I am thankful to know my God is a forgiving God. He knows that I can say something in error, and asks that I correct that error. He knows I can be caught in a temptation and can sin, and asks that I repent. He recognises that in a moment of frustration, I can speak unkindly, and he asks that I apologise.

The holy life is sharpened by our interaction with others. How we respond is the key. If we allow pride to stop us from apologising, or repenting, we fail God and disobey his voice. The Holy Spirit was sent into this world to teach us and guide us. Our task is to obey his voice. We are the ones who turn away from his power to triumph over sin. He is the one who brings us back to the feet of Jesus.

To pray:

Lord, I know you can keep me above sin today. Thank you! Should I sin, Lord, I will obey your voice to repent and put things right as you instruct me. I choose holy living today!

51

Myth 8 – Holiness Requires a Sensational Event

*'But you will receive power when the Holy Spirit comes on you;
and you will be my witnesses in Jerusalem, and in all Judea and
Samaria, and to the ends of the earth' (v. 8).*

I must admit that the night the Holy Spirit sanctified my soul – set me apart to serve him totally and cleansed me from inward sin – was one of the happiest nights of my life. Was it a sensational event? Yes. I had such a deep peace in my soul. Did I gain a special gift? Yes. I gained the Holy Spirit in his fullness.

However, there are many people who demand that sanctification be qualified by the ability to speak in tongues or other special gifts or manifestations of the Holy Spirit.

In Acts 1–3 we find the disciples of Christ were visited by what looked like fire and given the ability to speak in languages understood by those who knew those languages. In Acts 9 Paul received his sight. However, in Acts 1:8 we see that Jesus promised two things: power and becoming a witness.

Holiness is a changed heart. A holy heart is a heart free from envy about another person's ministry, free from jealousy because someone else has a new house and I don't, free from pride that says, 'Look at my life and see how well I am doing.' Sensational moments come and go, but the Holy Spirit's work in one's soul is sure.

We all have different personalities and God responds to those personalities. Some people are changed in a simple moment of faith and are never the same again. However, they have no memory of an emotional event or special gift given them.

Let's not judge God's way or means of sanctification. Let's trust him to keep his promise to sanctify us and prepare us for heaven. His Holy Spirit teaches us and guides us. He will not fail us!

Myth 9 – Holiness is Living Incarnationally or Answering a Particular Calling

'If I give all I possess to the poor and surrender my body to the flames, but have not love, I gain nothing' (v. 3).

Jesus is our great example of incarnational living (accepting simple living in order to identify with the needs of others). But there are those today who believe living like this is their holiness, instead of a humble heart changed by the Holy Spirit. Others believe that if they answer God's vocational calling, that particular surrender sanctifies their entire life. But pursuing a calling does not make one holy – submission of one's heart to the Holy Spirit does.

A dedicated church member purchased a used car, and to prove that he had no pride he painted several areas of it with very ugly paint. How sad! Such a person might make a great issue about his incarnational lifestyle; however, his self-satisfied example strikes observers as the pride of a Pharisee. This boast of humility actually reflects arrogance, and as a result such Christians forfeit an effective Christian witness.

The Holy Spirit makes a radical change in our hearts. Yes, we may choose to live a more frugal lifestyle, but that is not required to define our witness. When the Holy Spirit is in full control, his seal is on our lives and those around us find his presence quite evident in our words and actions, without our resorting to displays of 'sacrifice'.

Our key verse speaks of a sacrificial life that is empty of true change. Chapter 13 makes a perfect check-list for setting goals for holy living. The Holy Spirit waits for the invitation to mould and recreate us in his image. Are we willing?

———————

To pray:

Lord, I know you want me to live out 1 Corinthians 13, but it does not seem possible to live up to this list. Holy Spirit, I ask you to convict me in the area I most need to change. I bow to your will and your way.

Strength, Song and Salvation

'The LORD is my strength and my song; he has become my salvation' (v. 14).

Psalm 118 is one of the six psalms that comprise the *hallel* group (Psalms 113–118). All six were sung as one grand hymn at the Feasts of Tabernacles, Passover and Pentecost. Psalm 118 has an upbeat, trusting tone and is also prophetic of the Messiah. Jesus would have sung some or all of the verses just before going to the Garden of Gethsemane (Matthew 26:30). Consider what the psalm would have signified to him that night.

The psalm was one of Martin Luther's favourites. How it must have encouraged him when he faced opposition for his faith. He said, 'This is the psalm that I love . . . for it has often served me well and has helped me out of grave troubles, when neither emperors, kings, wise men, clever men nor saints could have helped me.'[15]

The psalm's structure suggests that it was used antiphonally in temple worship with part of the choir giving the first line and the other part responding with the second. In verses 1 to 4 the psalmist (probably David) enjoins the people, the priests and devout people everywhere to express thanks to the Lord for his steadfast loving-kindness. The poet goes on in verses 5 to 13 to give illustrative testimony to God's enabling strength.

Our key verse comes from the Song of Moses (see Exodus 15:2). It sums up the important reminder that although God often does amazing things for us, our hope is not in those demonstrations, however wonderful, but in God himself: 'The Eternal is my strength, of him I sing, he has delivered me indeed' (Psalm 118:14, *JMT*). In times of weakness, we can cling to the cross, wrap our sagging spirits around the unchanging righteousness of our Saviour and know his enabling victory.

Beyond the poem's limits, of the times and the political or military victories it describes, is the timeless strong deliverer who offers us spiritual victory out of defeat and life out of death. No wonder his people rejoice at such a day (v. 24). Thanks be to God!

Exercise 1 – Sing!

*'After consulting the people, Jehoshaphat appointed men to sing to the
LORD and to praise him for the splendour of his holiness as
they went out at the head of the army, saying: "Give thanks to the
LORD, for his love endures for ever" ' (v. 21).*

We have long understood the importance of exercise for our bodies, but do we consider the need to make holiness a part of our daily spiritual life? We will consider a few daily exercises that will keep us fit spiritually. Today, we look at singing.

In our key verse, we find Jehoshaphat appointing men to sing to the Lord and to praise him for his holiness. Our holy God has inspired words to songs that touch our hearts and urge us to holy living. When facing defeat, we can find victory in song. God-inspired songs call us to a higher life of purity.

Consider the holiness section of a Christian hymnal or Salvation Army songbook. Look for the key phrases that place that particular song in the holiness section. Ask God to speak to you through the hymns of our faith and heritage.

Hear the words of Catherine Booth-Clibborn: 'Weary I am of inbred sin, O wilt thou not my soul release? Enter and speak me pure within, Give me thy perfect peace' (*SASB* 450). Read the words of Bramwell Booth: 'O when shall my soul find her rest, my strugglings and wrestlings be o'er? My heart, by my Saviour possessed, be fearing and sinning no more? . . . O Saviour, I dare to believe, Thy blood for my cleansing I see; and asking in faith, I receive salvation, full, present, and free' (*SASB* 454).

Be challenged by the words of Albert Orsborn, 'Believe him! Believe him! The holy one is waiting to perfect within you what grace has begun; God wills for his people an uttermost salvation; to sanctify you wholly the Spirit will come!' (*SASB* 410). Consecrate yourself with the words of Herbert Howard Booth, 'Let the blood of Christ forever flood and cleanse my heart within, that to grieve thee I may never more stain my soul with sin' (*SASB* 502). Amen and amen!

Exercise:

Read a holiness song in its entirety today.

Exercise 2 – Scripture Reading

*'For wisdom will enter your heart, and knowledge will be
pleasant to your soul' (v. 10).*

We live in an information age. The radio, television, newspapers have been with us for years, but now the internet provides instant information about any issue, word or subject. Information and knowledge are good but mixed with them are the ungodly, the unholy and the lure to sinful living. In all the information you have read or heard this week, when did you hear a call to holy living unless you searched hard for it?

In Proverbs 2 we learn that it is our duty to be informed and search for the knowledge of God. 'If you call out for insight and cry aloud for understanding, and if you look for it as for silver and search for it as for hidden treasure, then you will understand the fear of the LORD and find the knowledge of God' (vv. 3–5). If we truly want to know the way of holiness, we must ask the Holy Spirit to guide us into this truth. We will read the Scriptures searching for examples of holy lives and the call to a holy living.

Unholy living is advertised, televised and encouraged all around us. The holiness exercise challenge today is to surround ourselves with holiness quotes and holiness books that will draw us towards holy living.

Build a holiness library. Consider William Booth's book *Purity of Heart*. Read *The Way of Holiness* by Samuel Logan Brengle. Keep John Wesley's *Christian Perfection* at hand. Find books by today's authors, including *New Love* by General Shaw Clifton. Keep these easily accessible. Read a paragraph or a chapter just to feed your soul with the doctrine and principles of holy living. Counteract the lure to unholy living with a search for keys to holy living.

Exercise:

Post one holiness quote in a familiar place where you can read it daily.

Exercise 3 – Psalms

'Create in me a pure heart, O God, and renew a steadfast spirit within me' (v. 10).

When we purchase 100 per cent natural honey we know it should not have peanut butter or jelly in it. Pure natural honey is only honey. However, if we look closely, pure natural honey could have a bit of beeswax in it, yet we still consider it pure honey.

David called for God to create in him a pure heart. This is a heart free of sin. David had fallen a long way from the young man fighting a giant by God's help to the king choosing adultery and murder. He knew he needed forgiveness, but he wanted more. He wanted God to provide him with a heart that was not only washed, but perfected. He needed a great God.

David wanted a heart free from chosen sin. True followers of Jesus don't lie, steal or cheat. We turn from the sin of adultery. We fight against the temptations that Satan brings our way. We respect our co-workers, and we are happy when they succeed. We can do this because God has recreated in us a clean, pure heart that loves him and loves others. This love is God-given.

Yes, we will have disagreements, hurt, pain and anger – some beeswax, if you will. However, the Holy Spirit is quick to call us to himself and forgives us when we ask him. He teaches us to apologise and promptly make peace with others. He leads us to forgive those who hurt us. He cleanses us and keeps on cleansing us as long as we remain obedient to him.

David lost his way but he knew the way back to forgiveness and holy living. God can lead us back, too, if we ask him.

———————

Exercise:

Read through the Psalms and find references to pure, clean, perfect.

Exercise 4 – Talk the Walk

*'"Love the Lord your God with all your heart and with all your soul
and with all your strength and with all your mind"; and
"love your neighbour as yourself"'* (v. 27).

Jesus was open to discussion. Consider what happened when people
gathered around him asking questions. He let them ask. People found
Jesus approachable. Let's look at his open discussion in Luke 10.

To the question, 'How can I inherit eternal life?' Jesus' answer takes us
to the heart of holiness: love God and love your neighbour. Easily said but
not so easily done if my neighbour is difficult to love. The final answer to
the question of eternal life is mercy. Be merciful to those around you who
are hurting. What started as an eternity question became an examination
of daily living. Jesus prescribed loving the unlovable and showing mercy to
those around us.

Too often, we memorise the doctrine of personal holiness, question its
possibility and place it back on the shelf. We do not wrestle with the truth
of the Bible on the subject, and therefore we do not allow the Holy Spirit
to guide us in actual holy conduct and intention. The Church must wrestle
together as we face this challenge. We *can* overcome wilful sin! If we
confront each other in an honest and openly accountable setting we will
eventually embrace this victorious way of living.

Early in my teaching of Salvation Army officer cadets in Russia I
thought my task was to teach them facts about holiness, holy living and the
work of the Holy Spirit. But I soon realised that my best teaching involved
listening and allowing them a safe place to voice their fears and questions
about holiness. Only then did they begin to believe it possible for them.

Exercise:

Establish a holiness discussion group online or in your home. Be bold! Don't fear
the discussion. Trust the Holy Spirit to guide you.

Exercise 5 – Holiness to the Lord

'Make a plate of pure gold and engrave on it as on a seal:
HOLY TO THE LORD*' (v. 36).*

If you enter a Salvation Army meeting hall you might see a holiness table. It is generally centred in the front of the worship area and may be covered with a velvet cloth with the words 'Holiness unto the Lord' written on it. It is a reminder that God calls us to excellence. He calls us to a life higher than that of daily sin.

Your attention might then be drawn to a simple bench placed carefully where people can kneel to pray. This is called the mercy seat. Here, through prayer, people can gain God's mercy for their sins and seek the power to conquer weakness that leads to sin.

Nearby you will find a tricolour Salvation Army flag. Red represents the blood of Jesus who died for our sins. The yellow of the flag stands for the Holy Spirit sent to us by Jesus. Blue indicates the God-like purity we can have through his Holy Spirit.

Should you pick up our songbook, you might open it to the sections entitled 'The Life of Holiness' or 'The Holy Spirit', each with songs that call us to a holy life. Perhaps you might pass by the library and pick up one of the many books written by Commissioner Samuel Logan Brengle, who wrote prolifically about holiness. Maybe you will participate in the Sunday morning meeting, called the holiness meeting.

At God's command, the priests of the Old Testament wore the words 'Holiness to the Lord' on their garb. Holiness has been a feature throughout the history of The Salvation Army; we cannot ignore it or keep it on the shelf for reference purposes only.

___

Exercise:

As you attend worship this week, ask God to show you his holiness. Make your daily motto, 'Holiness unto the Lord'. It is a call to excellence as we brush shoulders with our neighbours in our daily life.

Exercise 6 – Study Holiness!

*'Do your best to present yourself to God as one approved,
a workman who does not need to be ashamed and who correctly
handles the word of truth' (v. 15).*

Fishing and frog-catching take time, patience and skill. Not any worm will work to catch the biggest fish in the pond, and you can't fish at just any time of the day and expect the best results. Patience and understanding are important skills for catching fish. Catching frogs takes the skill of slow, careful, precise, direct planning. I spent many youthful hours catching fish and frogs. My father was a great teacher. Fish and frogs were mine for the taking if I took the time to catch them, but I first had to study them and understand their way of life.

An occasional Sunday sermon on holiness is helpful and may catch our attention, but serious study of God's word in search of understanding holy living takes slow, careful, precise, direct planning and searching with the Holy Spirit as our teacher. When we search God's word with honest, open hearts, he teaches us how to live this holy life that seems so impossible. Step by step, day by day, we learn, we grow; we gain an understanding of his grace, his mercy, his holiness and his call to holy living.

Perhaps you fear what you will discover. Let me assure you that God is greater than that fear. He is able to open his word to you. Perhaps you are too busy. In our key verse we are called to study the word of God. Let it be one of our daily exercises in holy living! With the Holy Spirit as our teacher, we will learn the deep truths.

Exercise:

Establish a holiness Bible study. Your soul will confirm the doctrine's validity and wake to the work of the Holy Spirit in your life.

Limitless Vision

*'May the God of hope fill you with all joy and peace as you trust
in him, so that you may overflow with hope by the power of the
Holy Spirit' (Romans 15:13).*

One of the six psalms comprising the eighty-five verses of the *hallel*
group is today's – a doxology. Some scholars think the psalm is a
fragment and should be attached to Psalm 116 or 118. Others argue that
it can certainly stand alone.

It is the shortest psalm and chapter in the Bible. Perhaps a two-verse
psalm is appropriate for February, the shortest month in the year. In the
New International Version it has few enough characters to stay under the
maximum Twitter limit of 140 (and even fewer in *The Message*).

How much can fewer than thirty words say? Ernest Hemingway's full
story in six words: 'For sale: baby shoes, never worn'; or six-word memoirs
such as 'Enter left. Move centre. Exit right'[16] illustrate that haiku-like
statements can convey much with little. We might recall hearing single-
sentence testimonies such as 'Saved and kept by God's grace'. Such brief
declarations can be challenging to create, yet a good exercise in concise
expression of important truths.

After reading today's psalm a few times – possibly in several versions –
we begin to see its depth. One scholar helps us when he says of Psalm 117:
'It is in the truest sense a Messianic Psalm and is quoted by Saint Paul in
Romans 15:11 as one of the Scriptures which foretold the extension of
God's mercy to the Gentiles in Christ.'[17]

In Romans 15:7–13 Paul articulates Christ's coming for the Jews in
confirmation of God's promises to his people. Thereafter they could glorify
God for his truth fulfilled. Because of the same gospel, non-Jews can
glorify God for his mercy which included us. Paul says that since Christ
accepted us, we need to accept one another – all to bring praise to God. As
we trust him who is the hope of the world and whose creative love
demonstrates hope, his Spirit fills us with his joy, peace and hope.

Exercise 7 – Seek Him!

*'My soul yearns for you in the night; in the morning my spirit longs for you.
When your judgments come upon the earth, the people of the world learn
righteousness' (v. 9).*

World-views surround us in numerous forms. The Christian world-view is vastly different from the Marxist, the humanist or the postmodernist. The Christian world-view is based on the belief that there is one God and that Jesus Christ died for our sins. Many believe this on Sunday, but during the week they brush shoulders with those who scoff at the idea of God. Gradually God becomes less important and distant. Then God becomes merely a possibility and eventually non-existent.

God's view must be our view if we are to make heaven our home. This comes only by seeking him daily. Isaiah cries out to God: 'My soul yearns for you in the night, and in the morning my spirit longs for you!' To keep this hunger, we must invite him to renew us daily by his Spirit. Without his renewing in our lives, the world calls us away from his view, and soon we have no understanding of sin. We become in sync with a world that no longer believes in God, in heaven or hell.

One of my father's regular questions to each of us children was: 'Are you ready for heaven?' No matter how committed to God I was when he asked the question, it made me stop and think: 'Am I all God wants me to be? Am I holy in his sight? Am I ready for heaven?' Eternity awaits us. Let us seek him daily!

Exercise:

Seek the Holy Spirit on a daily basis; ask him to continue to cleanse you and work through you. Listen to his quiet inner whisper as he guides you in the direction he wants you to take in your ministry, your interpersonal relationships and your daily life. Remember, God wants us to succeed in holy living.

Life, Light and Love

First Epistle of John

Introduction

Although 1 John is considered an Epistle, it is a different type of letter from others in the New Testament. It even differs from the apostle's two single-chapter letters (which we considered in July 2010). It has no opening address or closing greeting. It is more along the lines of a personal essay or message written with big themes.

John uses a caring, fatherly tone as he refers to his readers as his 'dear children' a number of times.

He writes the letter in Ephesus, before AD 100, probably not long after writing the Gospel of John. The style, vocabulary and ideas are similar in both. Scholars tell us that John's Gospel and this Epistle are so connected that questions suggested in one are answered in the other.

In the first century, some tried to improve on essential Christian teaching by fusing it with the Greek philosophy of Gnosticism, prevalent in the day. In this Epistle, John counters key points of the heresy as he concisely treats a number of vital Christian beliefs and repeatedly states what Christians '*know*'. Since everything depends on who God is and who Jesus is, John starts there. Then he presents the importance of confession of sin, atonement, cleansing and holiness as the basis of fellowship with God.

John speaks from a long life of experience in the Christian way, personal remembrance of Christ's teaching, encounters with the Risen Lord and knowledge of other New Testament books. Essentially his Epistle asks three important questions that build on each other: do we believe Jesus is the Son of God? Do we live righteous lives; and do we love one another?

The Word of Life

'Our motive for writing is simply this: We want you to enjoy this, too.
Your joy will double our joy!' (v. 4, MSG).

Before they respond to Jesus' call to be his disciples, John and his brother James are fishermen with their father, Zebedee, and very likely partners with Peter. Jesus calls the brothers, 'Sons of Thunder'. At times the apostle is shown to be boisterous, selfishly ambitious, intolerant and bold. Yet John is one of the three whom Jesus takes into special confidence on such momentous occasions as the raising of Jairus' daughter, Jesus' transfiguration and Jesus' final prayer time in the Garden of Gethsemane.

John accompanies Jesus throughout his ministry. He is at the cross where Jesus entrusts him with his mother Mary's care. John visits the empty tomb on Easter morning. He encounters the resurrected Christ in Jerusalem and in Galilee.

He is in the upper room on the day of Pentecost. In the book of Acts, John always appears with Peter, his boldness now turned to courage. Paul mentions John only once, but it is as one of the three pillars of the Church along with Peter and James.

At a mature age John sets down his Gospel, Epistles and the Revelation, which all emphasise the deity of Christ. His words exhibit gentle love. In 1 John he urges believers to rely on the Spirit and demonstrate love to God through obedient, righteous living and practical love for others.

John speaks fervently and lovingly to his readers, whom he does not name but with whom he seems well acquainted. In verse 1 John boldly declares that he has seen, heard and touched the Word of Life (Christ). Verse 2 is a parenthetical statement which emphasises the life which people could only *know* because it was revealed by Christ. The Word of Life was with the Father and is eternal.

In verse 3 John gives his primary purpose of writing. He wants believers to share that special fellowship he *knows* with God and his Son, Jesus Christ – best understood in terms of eternal life.

In His Light We See Light

'This is the message we have heard from him and announce to you, that God is light, and in him there is no darkness at all' (v. 5, NASB).

When John uses the title 'Word of Life' he is speaking of Jesus Christ, God incarnate. In today's Scripture he ties the eternal Word and life with the absolute light. God is light in his splendour, in his self-revelation, in his purity and holiness, in his illumination of our way, in his disclosure of our sin.

Darkness is the antithesis of light. It represents the ignorance, confusion, deceitfulness, decay and lovelessness of the Christless life and is the realm of the enemies of Christ.

John counters the claims of those who allege to be so spiritually superior that sin is insignificant or irrelevant to them. He says that staying in fellowship with the God of light means intentionally and continually maintaining a right relationship with him or, as some versions express it, 'doing the truth' (v. 6). There is more to Christianity than intellectual assent: what we believe can be seen in what we do.

John says that 'doing the truth' creates fellowship with others of like mind and keeps us aware of the sacrifice of Christ. If we want to be like him and to please him, we *know* that we need to rely on him to cleanse us and fit us to serve him day by day.

John has strong words for those who claim to love the Lord, yet live lives of wilful disobedience. John says that's lying. John also speaks out against those who say they have no responsibility for their sin, those who say their sins bring no harm and those who don't realise that they've sinned. John says that's self-deception. Only humble confession of sin can bring forgiveness.

But coming to God in penitence isn't an iffy proposition. God is true to his promise to forgive our sins. And on top of that, God cleanses us from the inclination to sin. 'He won't let us down; he'll be true to himself. He'll forgive our sins and purge us of all wrongdoing' (v. 9, *MSG*).

Test of Obedience

'Anyone who claims to be intimate with God ought to live the same kind of life Jesus lived' (v. 6, MSG).

In chapter 2 John builds on what he said about sin and forgiveness at the end of the previous chapter. Some might be tempted to think about sin flippantly since it permeates humanity and God's forgiveness is so readily available. So in a pastoral, fatherly tone John says he's writing that followers of Christ may not sin. If we *know* the Lord, we should want to obey him. If we are united to him, we should want to be like him.

But, says John, if we succumb to sin, we have an advocate (*parakletos*) with God – Jesus Christ. Jesus stands beside us and represents us to God as one fully equipped to plead a case in court. John uses the same word in his Gospel when he records that Jesus promises 'another advocate', meaning one like himself. He refers to the Holy Spirit (John 14:16) who counsels and advises us of a right course and the true way of thinking, the Jesus way.

Besides being our advocate with God, Jesus, the righteous one, is the atonement for our sins, the basis of our reconciliation to God. Out of great love for humanity, God sends Christ to redeem us, to provide the way of our return to the waiting Father, to offer forgiveness if we are penitent and willing.

John adds that God's remedy for restoring believers is the same as the provision that brought us pardon and salvation – the blood of Christ – and is on offer to the whole world to accept or reject.

John says that the evidence of *knowing* fellowship with God is our obedience to his word. We may admire those with great intellect. The Greeks who esteemed rational thought as the path to spiritual illumination might speak of solving the problem of God. Others tried to become one with divinity through emotional, mystical experiences. But John makes it clear that for Christians, *knowing* God comes through obeying God's revealed truth and in emulating Christ. Our intellect and emotions can then serve God through our loving, Christlike actions.

Enough Loaves to Share

'They will eat and have some left over' (v. 43).

A family friend from Germany remembers the long hours and hard work in her father's local bakery. As in many countries where large home ovens aren't common, the townspeople rely on the shop for their daily loaves of bread. Many cultures do not require loaves of bread as a staple of their diet, but often incorporate a form of bread made in some way from regional grain.

The aroma of freshly baked bread from a commercial bakery in our area is its own excellent advertisement. Customers are welcome to fill their paper sacks from large bins of rolls and bagels constantly replenished by conveyor belts that lead from the enormous automated ovens. It's easy to get carried away and not know the answer to the checkout clerk's question, 'How many do you have?'

I'm writing today's thoughts more than a year ahead of time, so don't know what direction Christian women in Chile will take as they prepare material for World Day of Prayer and work out this year's theme: 'How Many Loaves Have You?' No doubt their Scripture passage will be from one of the Gospel accounts of the time Jesus fed more than 4,000 with seven loaves or more than 5,000 with five loaves.

Today's short passage from the Old Testament is a precursor of what the Lord would later do for thousands. It happens during a time of famine when food is scarce. From unidentified wild plants, the prophets in training concoct a stew that nearly kills them. When a man brings Elisha twenty hearty barley loaves, he orders them to be given to the 100 prophets because the Lord says to do so. God multiplies the bread and signifies that he will provide for his followers.

Acknowledging our limited resources helps us to see God at work. When we are responsive to God's direction to share our limited resources and obey him, he assures his provision for us, 'according to his glorious riches in Christ Jesus' (Philippians 4:19).

To pray:

Today we pray especially for God's provision throughout Chile and for those people still impacted by last year's catastrophic earthquake.

Old and New

'Your love for one another will prove to the world that you are my disciples'
(John 13:35, NLT).

In 1 John 2:1 the apostle addresses readers as 'little children' and now in verse 7 as 'dear friends' or, as some versions have it, 'beloved' (with its root related to *agape*). John's loving attitude flows through his letter, even during passages of correction.

In verses 7 and 8, what does he mean by a commandment which is both old and new? The commandment is old, but not in the sense of being worn out, aged or out of fashion; rather in the sense of being original and essential. The Old Testament law taught to love God with all one's being and one's neighbour as oneself. Jesus endorses it, renews it and expands on it.

It is new in that Jesus teaches his followers to love as he loves (John 13:34, 35). Then he demonstrates even greater love when he gives his life for us. His love extends to more than his neighbours; he loves sinners and his enemies. His love meets more than the minimum requirement, he loves sacrificially and eternally.

By the time John writes, what Jesus taught has been passed on through several generations of believers, so that now the new is old. Yet Christ's standard of love is shown ever new when Christians acknowledge the truth and allow God's Spirit to demonstrate Christlike love through us. In Jesus it is completely fulfilled. When his followers exhibit such love, it shows it continues to be true and relevant.

John reminds those who either once walked in the light, or who think they walk in the light yet evidently no longer do, that not loving others leaves us in the dark whether we know it or not. He says there is no twilight zone. The choice is day or night. Either we love others or we don't. We walk in the light or the darkness.

A bonus to loving others and living in light is that we don't need to stumble nor cause others to stumble. With hymnwriter Horatius Bonar we pledge, 'And in that light of life I'll walk till travelling days are done' (*SASB* 332).

He Hears Me

'Be at rest once more, O my soul, for the LORD has been good to you' (v. 7).

This psalm is a song of deliverance. As with other Scripture, it may be intended to be read on multiple levels. There is the context of the culture, history and literature of the day in which it is written; the context of the message of Scripture as a whole; and from the time of the life, death and resurrection of Christ, the context of hearing strains of the new song of his provision for our redemption echoing from the Old Testament. We can read at all of these levels without blurring the message.

Since no author is noted, there are several ideas about whose deliverance the psalm celebrates. If David writes the psalm, he may be reflecting on a specific rescue when his life was spared – such as when Saul who sought his life came to the mouth of the cave where David and his men were hiding (see 1 Samuel 24).

If the writer is a survivor of the Babylonian captivity, then the reference to a return to the 'land of the living' (v. 9) may signify a return to the Promised Land with opportunity to once again offer sacrifice in Jerusalem (v. 19).

Many commentators think the psalm is Messianic and that it describes the suffering, death and triumph of Christ, as if Christ himself is speaking. If that is the case, additionally, in verse 16 we might hear Jesus paying tribute to his mother's acceptance of and faithfulness to God's plan.

We know that 'All Scripture is inspired by God and is useful to teach us what is true and to make us realise what is wrong in our lives. It corrects us when we are wrong and teaches us to do what is right' (2 Timothy 3:16, *NLT*). So we can see the psalm as our own testimony of deliverance from physical or spiritual death as well.

Bearing all this in mind, perhaps we should read the psalm several times – as if David speaks, as if a returnee speaks, as if Christ speaks and as if we testify that he hears us (v. 1). More than anything, let us hear and obey the word of the Lord to us today.

What Do We Want?

'The world and all its wanting, wanting, wanting is on the way out –
but whoever does what God wants is set for eternity' (v. 17, MSG).

John seems to use a poetic, rhythmic form in verses 12 through 14. Whether John addresses readers as 'my children' because they came to Christ through him or they are young in the faith, in a sense he addresses all Christians. When he addresses fathers he means all those who are mature in the faith and when he writes to young men it is to all who have a vigorous faith.

He wants us to remember that to avoid the dangers of walking in darkness and to keep going in the light, our best protection is keeping what God has done for us in mind. Our sins have been forgiven as we have believed in the name of Jesus Christ. We *know* our Saviour and in fellowship with him we are learning more of him. Armed with the word of God and the power of his Spirit, we are standing firm and overcoming the evil one.

When John admonishes believers not to love the world, he isn't talking about shunning the human race that God loves and that Christ died for, nor about ignoring the beautiful planet God created. The world we aren't to love is everything that keeps people from turning to God, everything that is God's rival, the whole system which operates out of selfishness, greed or evil influence.

John says that whether we're enthralled by ambition or self-gratification, controlled by desire to possess the latest or showiest things, or inflated by self-importance and empty boastfulness, such egocentric love of the world squeezes out love for God and isolates us from him.

Because the early believers held that in Christ the kingdom of God has arrived for those who believe in him, but not for those who reject him, they drew an obvious distinction between the world and the Church. That line may be blurred today. The world which believers are not to love is the one which is self-destructive, anti-God and waning. Our focal point should be what pleases God and therefore increases and lasts for ever.

Live Deeply in Him

'Stay with what you heard from the beginning, the original message. Let it sink into your life. If what you heard from the beginning lives deeply in you, you will live deeply in both Son and Father' (v. 24, MSG).

In the context of our day and culture we need to work out how to seek what pleases God instead of what a world opposed to righteousness tells us we should seek. What practical steps can we take? Some will nourish their wonder of God's goodness through beauty in art, music or nature; the wonder of God's grace through Scripture, prayer, worship and the testimonies of other believers.

When John says it's the last hour (v. 18) he may or may not be saying the end of the world or even the return of Christ is imminent. Obviously it was not. John probably means that because of increased persecution and martyrdom of Christians, a time of considerable crisis is at hand before a divine victory.

In a sense every age is 'the last hour' as the struggle between good and evil continues. We each have daily opportunities to choose to ally ourselves with the old world which will one day end or with the new world which is eternal. The term 'the last hour' is unique to this Epistle, although in his Gospel John repeatedly uses a similar term – 'the hour' – to mean a critical season.

Only John uses the term antichrist. It can mean one who opposes Christ or one who sets himself up in place of Christ while denying him. John's unique view of antichrist is not of a single individual, but of the power of evil working through false teachers who distort the truth and intentionally try to plant the distortion in people's minds. John says that such false teachers are Christians in name only and that they are sifted out when they leave the fellowship (v. 19). Anyone who denies that Jesus is Christ denies the Father and the Son and is antichristian (v. 22).

But John reassures true believers that even the humblest of us *knows* the truth: 'the holy One has given you his Spirit, and all of you *know* the truth' (v. 20, *NLT*). We affirm and abide in the truth that Jesus is the Son of God; Jesus is the Christ; Jesus is Lord.

These Things I Know

'I know whom I have believed, and am convinced that he is able to guard what I have entrusted to him for that day' (2 Timothy 1:12).

John assures us of things we *know*. He says that we're not only called God's children, we actually are. All human beings owe their existence to God, so in that sense are his creation, but only those who personally respond to the grace God initiates through his offer of salvation are truly his children.

Being a child of God has its privileges. Life as we know it is only the beginning. One day we will see the Lord. Not only will we have the satisfaction of recognising who he is, but when we see Christ, we will be like him. Yet Jesus tells us that only the pure in heart see God (Matthew 5:8). That isn't an impossible dream. His Holy Spirit will cleanse and keep us pure if we want that purity and ask for it. The great hope of seeing God motivates us to avoid sin.

John writes to counter the fallacy of the various arguments of the Gnostics (knowing ones) that sought to justify sin. They said that since the body doesn't matter, satisfying its lusts doesn't matter. They said that in their quest for knowing everything, they should try everything – good or evil – to expand their knowledge base.

John is clear that sin is breaking God's law, flouting one's own desires and disobeying God's commandments. Sin seeks to undo the work of Christ. Sin enters when we don't abide in Christ. Perpetual sin is of the evil one. But Christ faced and broke the power of evil.

John says that based on personal faith in divine revelation, believers *know* a number of things. We *know* that Jesus, the one without sin, came to take away our sin. We *know* that Christ can help us be victorious over sin. We *know* that with the word of God in our hearts, we can be kept from perpetual sin. And we *know* that those who live righteously and love other believers are children of God while those who don't are not his children.

So we pray with songwriter Albert Ernest Dalziel for 'a faith that answers firmly: these things, these things I *know*' (*SASB* 6).

Rest Assured

'We must believe in the name of his Son, Jesus Christ, and love one another, just as he commanded us' (v. 23, NLT).

John reminds us that from the beginning believers have been told to love each other. By 'the beginning' he might mean from the time Jesus was on the earth and taught his followers the imperative of love. Jesus said he'd loved them as his Father loved him. Further, he told them to love each other. It would be what would distinguish them as his followers (see John 13 and 15). Love for other Christians remains the believer's distinguishing mark.

John says it's no surprise if those opposed to the kingdom of God hate us. But he emphasises that when we sincerely love other Christians we can be *certain* that we've crossed over from the sphere of death to the sphere of life. What sort of love is he speaking about? John points to Jesus' sacrificial love and tells us to imitate it by a keenness to share with others in practical ways.

This doesn't suggest a religion of works. Some of us are of a temperament which lacks confidence, doubts the effectiveness of what we do and is prone to false guilt. John says that we can *know* we're of the truth and can set our hearts at rest.

John urges us to remember that God *knows* our hearts and desires even better than we do. If we're in tune with him who surpasses us in love and knowledge, we can quieten our hearts, assured of his peace while staying attentive to his Spirit's promptings.

'Those who obey his commands live in him, and he in them. And this is how we *know* that he lives in us: We *know* it by the Spirit he gave us' (1 John 3:24). With that outlook and obedience to God's word, we can rest assured, live hopefully and with confidence.

———

To ponder:

'I know the one in whom I trust, and I am sure that he is able to guard what I have entrusted to him until the day of his return.'

(2 Timothy 1:12, NLT)

Our Incarnate God

'My dear children, you come from God and belong to God. You have already won a big victory over those false teachers, for the Spirit in you is far stronger than anything in the world' (v. 4, MSG).

John continues to emphasise the importance of right belief coupled with Christlike behaviour. Since John writes in part to counter Gnosticism and other false and delusional teaching infiltrating the Church, when he advises testing the spirits to see if they are of God or not, he gives basic criteria. People who acknowledge that Jesus is the Christ, and that he has come in the flesh, are of God. Since Gnostics considered matter evil and spirit good, they couldn't accept Jesus' incarnation. As far as they were concerned, God wouldn't take on flesh. If Christ was God, he couldn't be human.

But if Jesus didn't come as a human being, then how could people follow his example? How could he be the high priest who personally knows humanity's infirmities and opens the way to God? How could he save people, body and spirit? Or how could people be united with God?

But Jesus *is* both human and divine. John encourages his readers not to fear false teachers, but to remember that we *know* the freeing truth. We are victorious in Christ and are overcomers because, by his Spirit, God indwells us and confirms his word to our hearts.

We might expect that ideas which deny the deity or humanity of Christ come primarily from philosophies of other religions. But they do at times also crop up from within the Church when someone's untested yet plausible-sounding 'insight' gains popular approval even though it is heretical teaching. John dealt with an issue of his day, and his caution is fitting for ours as well.

Today's culture might accept Christ as human. But denying Christ as God can be a popular or pseudo-intellectual stance which allows people to avoid considering the truth. Even if people refuse to believe the truth, the truth remains and will be revealed and will prevail. In Christ, God still offers his love to all who dare to believe him and receive him.

Perfectly Visible Love

'But if we love one another, God dwells deeply within us, and his love becomes complete in us – perfect love!' (v. 12, MSG)

John urges us to keep loving one another, and then says that 'everyone who loves has been born of God and knows God' (v. 7). I've often wondered about that statement. Does it mean that every person who is zealous for country or cause, emotionally passionate for a sweetheart, affectionate towards family, or cherishes a spouse is born of God and knows God?

These emotions may have some elemental essence in common with God's love since, although not necessarily godly love, all love reflects God's love in some way. But this isn't what John is teaching. One version says that the child of God is the one 'who *truly* loves' (v. 7, *JBP*). We could think of water which is basic to and necessary for so much on our planet. Although water that is useful for the garden or fish pond might resemble what is potable, to stay healthy we need to drink what is *truly* pure.

Today's passage is tied to yesterday's, so is set in the context of the great proof of God's love and of the veracity of the Spirit's witness – Christ's incarnation. John says that real love is God sending his Son as a sacrifice for our sins (v. 10). It's *agape* love. It has to do with a well-intentioned principle, not a momentary emotion. It involves a desire for the highest good of others. It's invincible good will. It uplifts, shows mercy, strengthens, rewards and doesn't compromise.

In response to such love, our wills aren't crushed, but our hearts are broken over sin. We don't succumb to God's power, but surrender to God's incomparable love.

Jesus tells us to love as he has loved us (John 15:12). If we exercise that kind of love, it's of the Spirit of God. It may be risky, but if we love each other the way God loves us, the circle is complete and people see love – not our love to God or his love to us, but God's very nature of love. What an amazing challenge!

Now and Forever

'Not to us, O LORD, not to us but to your name be the glory' (v. 1).

The Salvation Army's poet-General, Albert Orsborn, wrote a song for the movement's centenary celebrations in 1965. It opens by declaring the reason for the Army's audible and visible victory rally:

> Not unto us, O Lord,
> But unto thy great name;
> Our trumpets are awake,
> Our banners are aflame,
> We boast no battle ever won;
> The victory is thine alone.
> (*SASB* 163)

The song starts with words of affirmation similar to Psalm 115:1. It properly shifts the focus away from any honour God's people may accrue and onto God and his glory – still helpful reminders today.

To further emphasise that we worship and give glory to the Lord of the universe, the psalmist (as do Isaiah and Jeremiah) contrasts inanimate, artificial idols with eyes, mouths, noses, hands and feet with the living God, our help and defence, who is not made in our image and actually hears and answers prayer.

Today, people in the West don't frequently see such idols but they are still entrenched in culture and prevalent in many parts of the world. Perhaps Western idols don't look human, but when we give our worship to anything instead of God, we're in the same situation. Christians in places where idols are commonly displayed appear counter-cultural when they declare their faith in God alone. The psalmist says that worshippers become like their gods (v. 8). That's fair warning for all of us.

Verses 9 to 13 encourage the people of God, their leaders and all sincere believers to trust in God who alone is our ultimate help. The familiar description of God as 'maker of heaven and earth' (v. 15) is first used here in Scripture. The Lord who rules the universe and entrusts the earth to us deserves our praise now and always.

The Love that Swallows up Fear

*'We know that we live in him and he in us, because he has
given us of his Spirit' (v. 13).*

God is holy, just and righteous but isn't called holiness, justice or righteousness. God is love. Love is the essence out of which his other
attributes flow. Similarly, in Galatians 5 Paul writes that the fruit of the
Spirit is love. The other eight attributes of joy, peace, patience, kindness,
goodness, faithfulness, gentleness and self-control are segments of the one
essence of love.

The simple statement, God is love, explains his gifts of our creation, free
will, constant care, redemption and eternal life.

Out of love, God created us for fellowship with him. Out of love, God
limited himself and allowed us to choose to respond to him. Out of love,
he doesn't fill us with petrol and send us off to see how far we could go on
a tank, but he accompanies us, recharges us, keeps a keen eye on our needs
and offers direction.

Out of love, God freely offers his costly remedy for our sin. Out of love,
God promises a final justice in an eternity which rights all temporary
wrongs of this life.

In today's passage John again tells us that Jesus brings life, restores our
lost relationship with God, is our Saviour and is the Son of God. These
facts help us to rely on and confidently respond to the love God initiated.

God's love drives out fear: 'There is no room in love for fear. Well-
formed love banishes fear. Since fear is crippling, a fearful life – fear of
death, fear of judgment – is one not yet fully formed in love' (v. 18, *MSG*).
Rather, as our key verse reminds us, God's Spirit confirms that we dwell in
God. Such assurance and peace is priceless. With songwriter Harry
Anderson we pray:

> Saviour, I want thy love to *know*,
> That I in love may be like thee;
> O let it now my heart o'erflow,
> And live thy life in me.
>
> (*SASB* 455)

Love That's Aware

*'The command we have from Christ is blunt: Loving God includes
loving people. You've got to love both' (4:21, MSG).*

John repeatedly and inextricably connects loving God with loving
people (4:7, 11, 20, 21, 5:1, 2). He boldly calls our love for believers a
testimony to our salvation: 'The way we know we've been transferred from
death to life is that we love our brothers and sisters' (3:14, *MSG*).

Conversely, John says that we prove we love God's children by loving
God and by keeping his commandments (5:2). Perhaps he means that our
awareness of the love we have for other Christians develops each time we
love God and do what he says. After all, God's commandments often deal
with how we treat others.

We aren't like the futuristic robotic boy in the film, *Artificial Intelligence*,
programmed to automatically show unconditional love. But when our love
responds to God's love and we're willing, God in turn strengthens us to do
what he asks, especially when it seems to be beyond us.

Corrie ten Boom, Dutch Christian, Holocaust survivor and author, who
travelled the world as a public speaker, returned to Germany after the war.
Her message in one church had been on loving our enemies and showing
forgiveness. Afterwards, everything she had taught seemed at stake. A man
waiting to greet her had been one of her harsh prison guards. He extended
his hand, said he'd become a Christian and asked for her forgiveness.
Corrie's arm wouldn't move. She had no forgiveness for him. So she
prayed that the Lord would pour his forgiveness through her and he did as
she reached out her hand.

Most of us have less-spectacular opportunities to express love for other
believers. Paul delivered loving gifts from Gentile believers to Jewish
believers in Jerusalem. In addition to expressly giving to the church or
missions, obedience to God's gentle nudging to show practical love to
others in the faith – whether around the block or at the next desk – may
help to accomplish his purposes.

Believers are Winners

'And who can win this battle against the world? Only those who believe that Jesus is the Son of God' (v. 5, NLT).

John boldly states that our faith in Jesus as the Son of God conquers the world. Those who believe that Jesus is the promised Messiah have this perpetual victory. Why is this faith so dynamic? It stems from belief in the Incarnation. Such a faith says that we believe God cares for humanity enough to miraculously enter it and take part in it. He knows us and he is with us. That heartens us.

Faith in Jesus as the Christ acknowledges that he endured the worst the world could deal out, even death on the cross, and did it for us. Faith in Jesus as the Christ says that we believe he rose again as victor over death. If we believe in him and what he has done for us, he can keep us victorious as well.

What does John mean when he says that Jesus came by water and blood (v. 6)? Some commentators think John refers to the water and blood that poured from Jesus' side on the cross (John 19:34). But most concur that the reference points to Christ's baptism and crucifixion.

Here John may be countering a Gnostic heresy. An educated contemporary of John's, Cerinthus, taught that Jesus was only a man until his baptism when 'the Christ' descended on him as a dove. After his ministry of preaching and miracles, 'the Christ' part – incapable of suffering – left Jesus to suffer and die alone. John corrects this view as he makes it clear that Jesus Christ's death is essential to our redemption and that Jesus is ever the Christ.

The many miracles Jesus performs attest to who he is; the Scripture witnesses to him; God testifies to Jesus' Messiahship on several pivotal occasions in his life. The Holy Spirit is visually present at Jesus' baptism when God verbally declares approval of his Son. Disciples hear God's voice at Christ's transfiguration. Bystanders hear God's voice in reply to Jesus' prayer that God would glorify his name. Even at his death, unique wonders testify to who Jesus is (Matthew 27:45–54). What a Saviour!

Have Life?

'These things I have written to you who believe in the name of the Son of God, that you may know that you have eternal life, and that you may continue to believe in the name of the Son of God' (v. 13, NKJV).

People's collaborative testimonies hold weight. In Matthew 18, when Jesus talks about dealing with differences he says that if speaking to a person privately doesn't work, take witnesses. He refers to the Old Testament directive that the testimony of two or three witnesses is basic to establishing a matter (Deuteronomy 19:15). If a triple human witness can confirm a fact, how much more a triple divine witness.

Besides the Spirit, and the water and the blood John already mentioned, in his Gospel various witnesses come together regarding Jesus. John the Baptist witnesses to who Christ is. Jesus' actions witness to who he is. The Father witnesses to who he is. The Spirit witnesses to who he is. When we believe in Jesus Christ and commit ourselves to him, the Holy Spirit confirms within our hearts God's testimony as to who Jesus is.

Essentially, God's testimony is that he's given us eternal life in his Son. If we have the Son, we have life – otherwise we don't (1 John 5:12). Only God fully possesses and inhabits eternity, so we can only *know* eternal life if we know God and abide in him. Only Jesus can show us the Father and bring us to him.

Near the end of his Gospel, John says his purpose in writing is for people to believe who Jesus is and have eternal life through his name (John 20:31). Now, near the end of his Epistle, John says he writes that believers may *be sure* that they have eternal life (1 John 5:13). Key words in the Epistle substantiate this: *know, assure, confidence, believe,* life, love and faith.

———

To ponder:

At the core of my life, what is certain and unshakable?

80

Praying His Way

'We can approach God with confidence for this reason: if we make requests which accord with his will he listens to us' (v. 14, NEB).

John follows up his declaration of his purpose for writing the letter – so that believers in Jesus Christ may be certain of eternal life – with an affirmation of assurance about prayer. Perhaps the two are tied. The word John uses for confidence in our key verse carries the sense of full freedom of speech. God allows such frankness and freedom. We come with nothing to conceal. If we sin, we can confess it, repent and claim forgiveness through Christ. Jesus says we can choose to remain in him, let his words take hold of us, and pray with assurance (John 15:7).

Jesus says he will do what we ask in his name (John 14:13, 14). This is not a secret formula. Jesus asks that we consider whether our prayers are the kind he would pray. Are they consistent with his tone, do they line up with his character and have the qualities we would expect in his prayers? By example Jesus teaches us to pray, 'Thy will be done.' Such prayer is asking God what he wants and intending to cooperate with it. John says we can be sure that God hears and listens to requests made in concord with his will (v. 14).

Part of the believer's privilege of prayer is intercession. Paul advises that prayer be made for people in authority over us. He prays for his readers and asks for prayer for his ministry. James says we should pray for physically sick believers. In his letter, John tells us to pray for believers who aren't well spiritually – those overtaken by sin.

Sometimes swept up by the moment, some people may sin unintentionally or unwittingly. Others sin deliberately and defiantly in spite of knowing it goes against God's will. What does John mean by a 'sin that leads to death' (v. 16)? Is it denying Jesus as Son of God, come in the flesh, and influencing others to do the same; or listening to sin and refusing to listen to God so often, that one loves sin? We don't know. And we don't know what is in another's heart. So we pray in faith as God prompts and leave the results to him to judge.

Hold to the True and Real

'We know that no child of God is a sinner; it is the Son of God who keeps him safe, and the evil one cannot touch him' (v. 18, NEB).

As John closes the Epistle he re-emphasises the certainty of what Christians *know*. Through Christ we *know* God; we *know* we have eternal life and everything we need for our spiritual life; we *know* that obeying God and loving other believers is essential; we *know* that the Holy Spirit's presence in our lives confirms that we are abiding in him.

As John closes the Epistle he re-emphasises the certainty of what Christians *know* to be fundamental. We have fellowship with God through Jesus Christ. Such fellowship with our Redeemer, Victor and Defender shields us from sin. Christ's grip on us keeps the evil one at bay (v. 18).

We *know* that being born of God and delivered from sin makes us opponents of whatever opposes God including the fallen, God-estranged world that lies in the evil one's clutches (v. 19). We *know* that Jesus, the Son of God, has come. In addition to bringing us redemption, he helps us understanding spiritual reality. He who is true is the one who helps us know truth: 'This Jesus is both True God and Real Life' (v. 20, *MSG*).

By contrast, John exhorts his readers to guard themselves from things that are not real – lifeless idols. This may sound strange until we recall that John writes from Ephesus, which in his day contained a lucrative centre of idolatry, immorality, lawlessness and superstition – the temple of Diana.

Such centres are still with us in new and alluring forms with appearances as up to date as the latest media or technology. So when John urges readers to hold to the real and true while protecting themselves against what isn't – 'Be on guard against all clever facsimiles' (v. 21, *MSG*) – he sounds a timeless warning to guard our hearts against everything that would usurp the Lord in our lives. God's Holy Spirit will help us if we ask him.

Greater than What the Sea Saw

*'Tremble, Earth! You're in the Lord's presence! in the presence
of Jacob's God' (v. 7, MSG).*

Although there is no title or author for today's psalm, which is one of the *hallel*, from its reference to Judah and Israel we might assume that it was written after the time of David. Some Bible scholars even attribute it to Shadrach, Meshach and Abednego, or Esther and Mordecai – all Jews who were faithful during their exile in foreign lands and who would have delighted in God's hand in history.

That could account for why this delightful psalm is original in its style. It doesn't use the conventional poetic language of other psalms. While it does extol the power of God, it does so in a unique way through crisp description of nature acting remarkably.

Nevertheless the writer uses some things conventional in Hebrew poetry. As are the segments of Psalm 119, the psalm is eight verses long. They comprise four stanzas of two verses each. The psalmist also uses parallelism: Israel and Jacob; Egypt and people of strange language; Judah and Israel; sanctuary and dominion; driving back the Red Sea and the Jordan River; mountains and hills; rocks and flint; pools and springs.

Nature responds to God's might and is witness to his miracles. The exodus grounds Israel in God's redemptive power. The Promised Land evidences the Lord's choice to dwell and reign with his people. We can draw parallels with New Testament teaching. The cross grounds us in God's saving power. The promised Holy Spirit shows the Lord's intention of dwelling and ruling in our hearts and in his Church.

The psalm appears to end abruptly but, as one scholar observes: 'The reader is left to draw for himself the natural and obvious conclusion, that the God, who thus drew water from a flinty rock for the supply of Israel, can still educe the richest blessings from what seem to be the hardest and most inauspicious situations.'[18]

God still delivers, provides and empowers. Hallelujah!

Glimpses of Glory

Selected portions from Revelation

Introduction

We've spent a fortnight with one of the apostle John's Epistles and we'll soon turn to his Gospel. Although we won't take time in this edition for a full study of his other contribution to Scripture, Revelation, for a few days we'll visit highlights from the book.

Writer:	John the apostle, in exile for preaching the word and for his testimony about Jesus.
Location:	Patmos, a small Greek island off the coast of Turkey in the east Aegean Sea. Tradition says that John received his vision while in a cave – which in some seasons could have been a welcome shelter.
Conditions:	If winter, chilly and rainy; if summer, hot and dry.
Companions:	None mentioned.
Daily activity:	Unsure. When the Romans controlled the area and used Patmos as a place of exile, the exiles worked the mines.
When:	John says it was on the Lord's Day. This is the first mention of this term in the New Testament. Even if he couldn't meet with believers, as was no doubt his practice in Ephesus, he would have observed the day in his heart.

As we consider John's writings, may we too know that 'God blesses the one who reads the words of this prophecy to the church, and he blesses all who listen to its message and obey what it says, for the time is near' (Revelation 1:3, *NLT*).

Divine Message

*'I, Jesus, have sent my angel to give you this testimony for
the churches' (v. 16).*

In both his Gospel and Revelation John presents extremes in conflict. In the Gospel we see light versus darkness, love versus hate, truth versus deception. In Revelation it is God warring against Satan. In contrast with John's Epistles and Gospel of a calm and deliberate nature, one scholar says of Revelation: 'The author writes in Greek, but thinks in Hebrew', which results in some grammatical irregularities and abruptness.

There may have been several contributing factors to the differences.

First, if John wrote his Gospel and Epistles in Ephesus, excellent Greek secretaries would have been available, but if he wrote Revelation while on his own on Patmos, he would have to write it in whatever level of Greek a Jew from Galilee knew.

Next, the subject matter of Revelation is different from that of the Gospel and Epistles. The visions John saw may have seemed indescribable.

Finally, the many visions and their descriptions are modelled after Old Testament prophetic style. One Bible translator notes that in Revelation there are nearly 300 references from Old Testament prophetic books including nearly seventy from Daniel, itself an apocalyptic book.

Chapters 1–3 (chiefly letters to seven churches) were commented on in the 2005 Pentecost edition of *Words of Life*. John's greeting indicates that the whole book is a letter addressed to the seven churches of Asia. There were of course more than seven churches. In Scripture, the number seven is often used to represent totality. The seven churches could represent the whole Church of the day. If they also represent aspects of the Church in every generation, the counsel is ever pertinent.

In the opening verses, John says the message is from God and urges readers to take it to heart (1:1, 3). In the closing verses Jesus himself affirms that he has sent his angel to give John this testimony for the churches (22:16). Are we listening to Jesus through his word today?

Glory to God

'All glory to him who loves us and has freed us from our sins by
shedding his blood for us' (v. 5, NLT).

In Revelation we may well notice some of John's signature phrases, style and concepts. John speaks of situations and people who witness to truth; of those who overcome; of keeping God's commandments; of the True and Real One; of Jesus, the Lamb of God, the Word (*logos*), the Light, the Life; of the efficacy of the blood of Jesus; of God's glory.

In his opening sentence, when John identifies the source of the book, he proclaims Jesus as Christ. In the same breath John mentions the word of God and the testimony of Jesus Christ (v. 2).

John says that the revelation is from Christ (v. 1). The Greek word for revelation is *apokalypsis* (apocalypse), meaning an unveiling or disclosure of something previously hidden or not understood. Luke uses *apokalypsis* in Simeon's song about Jesus as a God-revealing light to the Gentiles. Paul uses *apokalypsis* meaning God-given spiritual insight. He and Peter also use *apokalypsis* for the second coming of Christ when Jesus will be revealed in his glory.

Whereas an epiphany is a single event or divine appearance which reveals something, an apocalypse is more wide-ranging and may involve several 'appearings' or manifestations all meant to be contemplated and which taken together offer lasting insight.

Almost from the start, when John speaks of Jesus, he breaks into doxology. He praises Jesus for loving us; freeing us; making us priests – part of the redeemed kingdom of God over which he reigns. No wonder he exclaims: 'All glory and power to him forever and ever!' (v. 5, *NLT*). We pray with Salvationist poet Harry Read:

> Lord of all glory and of grace;
> Lord of all nations, worlds and space,
> Lord God o'er all eternity
> Reign thou – O reign thou over me.
> (*SASB* 957)

The Z and A

' "I am the Alpha and the Omega," says the Lord God, "who is,
and who was, and who is to come, the Almighty" ' (v. 8).

John turns to see who is speaking to him and sees a figure amidst seven lamp stands. In verses 14 and 15 the descriptive titles John gives of the one he sees remind us of some Old Testament terms for God. He applies them to the Risen Christ.

Compare the head and hair white as wool or snow with the description of the Ancient of Days in Daniel 7:9; eyes like fire and feet like burnished bronze with Daniel 10:6. Compare a voice like the sound of rushing waters with Ezekiel 43:2.

Is his face, like the sun shining in all its brilliance, similar to the shining presence of the glory of the Lord the Israelites saw on Mount Sinai (Exodus 24:17)? It also might well tie to John's experience on the Mount of Transfiguration when Christ's face shone as the sun (Matthew 17:2).

It isn't surprising that when John sees such a startling sight he is overwhelmed with reverential fear in the presence of the holy, glorious Risen Lord. The Lord touches John and says, 'Do not be afraid', just as he had on the Mount of Transfiguration.

In verse 8 Christ says he's the Alpha and Omega, the first and final letter of any alphabet – or as Dr William McCumber says of Christ: 'As the source and the goal, he brackets our existence.'[19] Now in verse 17, as if to underscore his statement in verse 8 and to further reassure the frightened apostle, Christ says, 'I am the first and the last.'

Near the end of an old pilgrimage route in northwest Spain someone spotted the Greek letters Ω A (Omega and Alpha) in the stone lintels above church doors. Was this a mistake? A few miles further on a rocky promontory juts into the ocean. It was once thought to be the westernmost edge of the earth, possibly the entrance to the place of the dead. Perhaps placing the letters in reverse order was to remind believers that Jesus is not only the first and the last, but also the last and the first, the starting point of a greater journey.

Open Door to Glory

'Holy, holy, holy is the Lord God, the Almighty – the one who always was, who is, and who is still to come' (v. 8, NLT).

We can only speculate whether the apostle carried a writing portfolio into exile, but somehow he has the equipment he needs. Although probably a new experience for him, John takes dictation as Christ instructs. He records the letters to the seven churches which comprise chapters 2 and 3 of Revelation. The letters deal with particular conditions, and give correction and commendation.

The principles of their messages remain relevant to the Church today. The concluding admonition in each – 'He who has an ear, let him hear what the Spirit says to the churches' (3:22) – includes each of us. All seven letters contain wonderful promises for those who stay true to Christ to the end. They extend to us. Excavating those promises and their significance would be a beneficial and encouraging study.

Even before John jots down Christ's missives to the churches, the Lord tells him: 'Write, therefore, what you have seen, what is now and what will take place later' (1:19). John's obedience brings us the book of Revelation. The command may well also assure that John will personally remember the details. Allowing a thought to run from our head to our hand and onto the page is a great aid to memory.

Now in chapter 4, John sees an open door and hears the voice that instructed him to write, a voice he knows as Christ's, issuing the clear, commanding invitation of a lifetime – to the throne room of God in heaven. As with all blessings of God's grace, this is intended to make him a better messenger of God's truth.

There are many descriptions in Revelation. Some might baffle us; others leave us dumbfounded. In chapter 4 John describes the breathtaking heavenly scene. We enjoy its splendour and majesty but, lest we get lost in the details, we remind ourselves that the focus of the book is the ultimate triumph of God in Christ. Then we join in worship of our holy, eternal Lord God Almighty.

The Lion is the Lamb

'Yet the divine and only Son, who lives in the closest intimacy with the Father, has made him known' (John 1:18, JBP).

In chapter 4 we see God seated on his throne surrounded by perpetual praise. In chapter 5 the focus is on Christ. When it distresses John that no one is able to open the sealed scroll and reveal its message, an elder consoles him. He assures him that there is one qualified to open the scroll and to explain and carry out God's purposes. John should not have been surprised.

While walking with the grief-stricken travellers to Emmaus on the first Easter, Christ had explained the Scriptures about himself and his mission. They told the disciples. Next, when Jesus reminded his disciples in Jerusalem that what was written about him in Scripture must be fulfilled and opened their understanding, John was there. Christ made it clear that they had witnessed his suffering and resurrection, which opened the way for repentance and regeneration in his name to be preached in all nations (Luke 24).

The elder who assures John about the scroll says that one has prevailed, triumphed, overcome by his incarnation, death and resurrection. He names him as the triumphant Lion of the tribe of Judah and the Root of David. Those titles for Christ would also resonate with John. Of course, the Christ who opened the disciples' understanding to Scripture would be the one who could not only open the scroll, but also explain it.

As John looks to the centre of the throne room, he doesn't see a lion but a lamb surrounded by the four living creatures and twenty-four elders. The Lamb appears to be slaughtered, yet stands tall. He takes the scroll from the Eternal One on the throne.

The tenor of the scene changes from sobbing to singing. Each of three songs is sung by more and more voices. One celebrates the worthiness of the Lamb; the next adds what God confers on the Lamb; the third unites the Lamb and the One on the throne. As we thoughtfully read these songs, we join the universal praise of 'the Lamb of God, who takes away the sin of the world' (John 1:29).

On Earth as it is in Heaven

'He who sits on the throne will spread his tent over them' (v. 15).

After John writes letters to the seven churches, he visits heaven's throne room. In chapter 6 he watches as, one by one, six of the mystifying scroll's seven seals are opened, some heralding devastating consequences on earth. Chapter 6 closes with a final question as to who is able to stand in the day of wrath.

Chapter 7 answers: those who are saved and sealed by the blood of Christ. Many commentators hold that rather than representing a specific limited number, the 144,000 (12 x 12 x 1,000) here and in 14:1–5 signifies a large complete host.

Now before the seventh and final seal of the scroll is opened, John portrays another wonder of heaven. It's not a select band of priests assembled, but an innumerable mass of people who from the world's nations, tribes, races and language groups come to God through Christ and stand in front of the Lamb and before God's throne. These appear not trampled, shabbily dressed, worn out or mumbling, but triumphant, white-robed, holding palm branches and crying out clear praises to God and the Lamb.

Those in the outermost ring of heaven's arena, the angels, now down on their faces, join the sevenfold praise in adoration of God: 'Praise and glory and wisdom and thanks and honour and power and strength be to our God for ever and ever. Amen!' (v. 12).

The saved serve God day and night and he dwells among them or spreads his tent over them (v. 15). Isn't this reminiscent of the way John describes the Incarnation: 'The Word became flesh and made his dwelling among us' (John 1:14)?

It also reminds us of Old Testament references to the visible presence of the Lord's glory with which God led his people, visited Mount Sinai, dwelt in the tabernacle and the temple. Isaiah (4:5, 6) and Ezekiel (37:27) prophesied of a day when God would dwell with his people and his glory would be a canopy to them.

Those of the Church on earth and in heaven who live for God's glory know the blessing of his presence.

'Lord, I Lift Your Name on High'

'From the rising of the sun to the place where it sets, the name of the LORD is to be praised' (v. 3).

As we continue to page backwards through the psalms, we come to the initial psalm of the *hallel* collection (Hallelujah Psalms). It starts with the instruction 'Hallelujah' or 'Praise the Lord'.

Verses 1 through 3 remind God's servants to praise the name of the Lord always and everywhere. The verses may remind us of the opening of the Lord's Prayer: 'Our Father in heaven, hallowed be your name. Your kingdom come. Your will be done on earth as it is in heaven' (Matthew 6:9, 10, *NKJV*).

The name of the Lord should be praised worldwide from rising to setting sun. What is more, in Scripture Jesus is himself called the Sun of Righteousness, as familiar Christian songs written through the centuries also remind us. In part of his prayer, 'The Rising Sun',[20] Salvationist songwriter Keith Banks addresses the Lord:

> Rising Sun;
> O Rising Sun,
> New morning song,
> Please make me strong.
> And let my lifeless, weakened soul
> Be whole.
> Then to your throne
> My own
> Sun will arise.
> Rising Sun, please shine on me,
> Fill me with your energy;
> As I pray, so let me be
> Touched by your divinity.
> Then clothed in splendour,
> Like a new day dawning,
> I'll thank you for the
> Glory of the morning.

Gentle Shepherd

'For the Lamb at the centre of the throne will be their shepherd' (v. 17).

The Lamb is central. The Son shares the Father's kingdom. We might think of a lamb as a harmless animal suitable for a children's petting farm. But this Lamb is the sacrifice for our sins. This Lamb is also a sovereign – the King, the Lion of the tribe of Judah (5:5).

And the Lamb is the Shepherd who leads the people of his flock to living water (literally, life's water-springs). He who sought us and paid for our salvation now guides us and will at last fulfil and satisfy our deepest longings.

We naturally think of Psalm 23. As well-tended sheep we confidently address our loving Shepherd with Salvationist poet Peter M. Cooke:

> Gentle shepherd, lead my feet
> Through pastures green to waters sweet.
> My soul revive, my steps restore,
> That I may love you more and more.
> When the dark veil of death I face,
> Support me still with words of grace.
> Protect me from unnumbered foes
> Which my heavenward way oppose.
> Then at last, dangers past,
> With the blest, let me rest
> Within the heavenly fold so fair,
> Gentle Shepherd, lead me there.[21]

We'll see the message of Revelation 7:9–17 appear again in expanded form in the two climactic closing chapters of Revelation when the Holy City is more fully described.

Our present experience of being saved, sealed and serving can be a foretaste of our future when the added dimension will be that it is without suffering.

Completely

'Heaven fell quiet – complete silence for about half an hour' (v. 1, MSG).

In the Old Testament the number seven often signified God's covenant with his people. We think of God setting apart the seventh day as holy, of the number seven in various rituals of purification and consecration, of the seven days God's people encircled Jericho before it fell, of Jewish feasts such as the Passover, the Feast of Tabernacles, the Sabbath-year, and the Jubilee organised by sevens.

The number seven recurs in the New Testament. The number often signifies completion or perfection. When Peter asks how many times he should forgive an offender Jesus replies seventy times seven – completely.

Both directly and indirectly, John frequently uses the number seven in Revelation. There are references to seven spirits before the throne, seven churches, seven golden lamp stands, seven stars in Christ's right hand, seven angels, seven horns and seven eyes of the Lamb, seven seals of the book, seven angels with seven trumpets.

We also note a sevenfold ascription of praise to God indicating perfection of power (5:12). Chapters 4 through 22 seem to consist of seven scenes revealed to John which culminate in the New Jerusalem.

In chapter 8, when the Lamb opens the seventh and final seal on the distinctive scroll, the unexpected reaction is an anticipatory silence in heaven. Until now, John describes a noisy place filled with sounds of trumpet and thunder and dominated by songs and praises. Suddenly as on cue, activity is suspended and everything is profoundly and perfectly silent in the ultimate dramatic pause.

What fills this breathing space is also remarkable: an angel bears a special aromatic offering to God at the altar of incense – the prayers of his people meant for God alone. Could heavenly activity truly halt to make way for God to hear our whispered prayers? How heartening that even in our extremity when we have little else to offer, God values and makes way for our prayers.

The Unshakable Kingdom

*'All who are victorious will inherit all these blessings, and I will
be their God, and they will be my children' (v. 7, NLT).*

Contrary to what we might expect, the elderly disciple's senses seem to be enhanced rather than diminished as he writes his report. The detail John communicates seems to be from 20/20 vision and unimpaired hearing. Whether John records disturbing or glorious scenes, he describes the indescribable as clearly as today's computer-generated virtual reality simulates the real world. John's record often carries multiple layers of messages.

Now in chapter 21 he conveys glimpses of the New Jerusalem as realistically as possible and in down-to-earth terms his first readers can understand. He sees an enormous golden translucent city 1,400 miles long, wide and high. He sees pearls and precious gems as gates and foundation stones. The glory of God illuminates the city; the Lamb is its light. The city is open to anyone from any nation whose name is in Christ's Book of Life.

The coming kingdom and the heavenly city, our inheritance and life of hope, our citizenship, our spiritual covenant and growth towards maturity, access to the Father, opportunities for faithfulness on the way all revolve around our relationship with Jesus Christ.

He was given authority, glory and sovereign power; all peoples, nations and men of every language worshipped him. His dominion is an everlasting dominion that will not pass away, and his kingdom is one that will never be destroyed. (Daniel 7:14)

Look up, and be alert to what is going on around Christ – that's where the action is. See things from *his* perspective . . . When Christ (your real life, remember) shows up again on this earth, you'll show up, too – the real you, the glorious you. Meanwhile, be content with obscurity, like Christ. (Colossians 3:2, 4, *MSG*)

So we focus on the certainties of Christ's unshakable kingdom and with renewed spirits worship him (Hebrews 12:28).

The Underlying Hope

'"Yes, I'm on my way!" Blessed be the one who keeps the words
of the prophecy of this book' (v. 7, MSG).

At the end of dozens of matches recently played in India, Sri Lanka and Bangladesh, this week four winning teams played in the semi-finals of the tenth Cricket World Cup. The 2 April final will determine the champions. The anticipation of four years mounts, then culminates in a victory on Saturday.

In North America, after spring training games, the beginning of April is the opening of the annual baseball season with ever-hopeful fans supporting their favourite teams and dreaming of a bid for the annual World Series championship six months away.

Whether we look for a victory in a few days, months or years, the very hope keeps us focused and helps to move us ahead towards the possibility. How much more does our hope in Christ and his sure promises stabilise us, especially through uncertain times? (Hebrews 6:18–20).

The events of Revelation are sometimes regarded as imminent, distant or symbolic. Even if we cannot fully understand Revelation or determine whether its primary significance was for John's times, is a continuous historical one, remains for the future or as some combination of these and other views, the essential message is clear, timeless and relevant to our generation.

Donald W. Richardson suggests:

The coming of the Lord is the dominant note of the book. 'Surely I come quickly' is the word of Christ to his suffering saints. That coming is a progressive and repeated coming. At many times and in many ways Christ comes. He comes when in faith we first turn to him; he comes in the crises of life when we call upon him; he comes in the hour of death to receive us unto himself . . . In the end, in the fulness of time, he shall come visibly in glory to close the scenes of our earthly history and to usher in the final judgment.[22]

Hallelujah!

Consider Christ

Selected chapters from John's Gospel

Introduction

Not long before Jesus went to the cross, he asked his disciples who people were saying he was. Their replies included John the Baptist, Elijah and a prophet. Then he asked who they thought he was. Peter's affirmation that Jesus was the Christ showed that the disciples had begun to understand his mission, but they still needed to learn what it really meant.

The situation and the question, 'Who do people say I am?' appear in Matthew, Mark and Luke, but not in John. However, John's Gospel repeatedly explains who Jesus is. Sometimes we're told by Jesus himself – in the 'I am' titles and other claims; sometimes by someone Jesus encounters; and sometimes by the Gospel writer. It isn't surprising that some of the titles John records in his Gospel tie with titles of Christ he records in Revelation.

There's another connection with John's other books. As with his Epistles, he writes the Gospel in part to counter the Gnostic heresy creeping into the Church in his day. He repeatedly asserts the deity and humanity of Christ. John frequently uses his characteristic word 'know'. With a strong appeal to Gentiles, John's Gospel is firmly rooted in Judaism.

The popular Bible commentator William Barclay calls John's Gospel an eagle eye view. John doesn't give us the lineage of Christ, his parables or as many of his miracles as the other Gospels do. He focuses on Christ's ministry in Jerusalem and Judea, not Galilee.

John is concerned with relating who Jesus is, what he teaches us about authentic spiritual life, and examples of what he does – all of which should prompt our faith in him. John's work is doctrinal and interpretive, the work of a contemplative.

After a lifetime of following Christ and being led by the Holy Spirit, John sets down not just what Jesus said, but what he now knows Jesus meant. As we read John's Gospel and rely on the Spirit's guidance, we will realise afresh with hymnwriter William Cowper:

> God is his own interpreter,
> And he will make it plain.
> (*SASB* 29)

Life and Light

'In him was life, and that life was the light of all people' (v. 4, TNIV).

Although none is exclusive, the synoptic Gospels primarily tell us of Jesus' ministry in Galilee, whereas John focuses more on Jesus' encounters in Jerusalem and Judea. The interwoven records give us a rich tapestry of the life of Christ.

John's way of portraying Jesus' ministry is different from Matthew, Mark or Luke's. In an art exhibition Matthew's might be a set of complete scenes, Mark's a collage of hastily captured pictures and Luke's an unfolding, detailed panorama, while John organises his presentation by themes.

From his large collection of facts, John doesn't try to write Jesus' biography. He presents a selection which best illustrates certain spiritual truths. John tells us as much at the close of the book (20:30, 31). Of the main recurrent themes in John's Gospel, the central message is that eternal life comes by believing that Jesus is the Son of God and Saviour of humankind.

In the Gospel of John a form of the word 'believe' occurs nearly 100 times and 'life' more than fifty. In the prologue (1:1–18) John mentions themes he plans to develop in the rest of the book: the Word, the Life, the Light, the Son, truth, witness, belief, power to become, being born of God, and fullness.

In chapter 1 John tells us that the Word is the source and principle of life. Here life doesn't merely mean physical existence, but quality, lasting spiritual life. Such life brings light or enlightens human beings. In whatever way Christ is at work in the world, he brings illumination and draws people to real, quality, abundant life.

William Barclay[23] comments that the light Jesus brings puts chaos and darkness to flight; reveals things as they truly are; and offers us guidance. Even in a world which turns its back on Christ in hostile darkness, his pure light shines on and is not extinguished.

One of a Kind

'We have seen his glory, the glory of the Father's one and only Son'
(v. 14, NLT).

John points us away from John the Baptist and to Jesus, the authentic light. This isn't to diminish the baptiser's mission and role but to be clear that they are subordinate to Christ's. Later the baptiser freely confesses that he is not the Christ (v. 20). In verse 8 John says that rather than being the light, the baptiser was a witness to the true light. He would bring people to faith in Christ.

When John writes that Christ is the true light (v. 9) he implies that by comparison other lights are insubstantial. A low-wattage bulb might keep us from bumping into things in the dark, but would never do as task lighting. Even an adequate reading light pales when compared with sunlight.

Jesus brings the blazing light of truth which dissipates doubt, despair and death. The Nicene Creed calls the Lord Jesus Christ 'the only-begotten Son of God . . . God of God, Light of Light, very God of very God'.

Christ, the *Logos*, who existed with God from before the beginning of time, participated in the world from its commencement (vv. 1–3).

The natural created world itself implies a Creator and should lead us to recognising him. Paul says as much in Romans 1:20.

When the *Logos* comes we have the perfect revelation of all God is and what he desires for us. Yet strangely, when Jesus Christ appears, the world does not recognise him. Furthermore, even though Jesus comes particularly to God's chosen people and land, many not only seem unprepared for him but reject him and his message.

Not everyone rejects Jesus. Some receive him and trust in who and what he is – the embodiment of the heart and mind of God. John tells us that such Jesus-embracing faith opens the way for ordinary people to become children of God. Praise God that the offer still stands. We who have seen his glory can help point others to the genuine Light of the world, Christ.

A Matching Set

'His miracles are his memorial – This GOD of grace, this GOD of love'
(111:4, MSG).
'Sunrise breaks through the darkness for good people – God's grace
and mercy and justice!' (112:5, MSG).

Psalms 111 and 112 are usually considered as a pair. This is in part because when taken together they form an acrostic psalm which uses all twenty-two letters of the Hebrew alphabet. They both begin with 'Hallelujah'. For that reason some commentators suggest that they may be the introduction to the *hallel* (Psalms 113–118).

Verses 1 through 8 are couplets and verses 9 and 10 are triplets in both psalms. Each line begins with a successive letter of the Hebrew alphabet. Besides their parallel form, some of the same words are used in both.

Another reason for reading them as a pair is that their subjects complement each other. Psalm 111 extols the character of Jehovah while Psalm 112 relates the character of one who follows the Lord. The first half of Psalm 111 praises God's works of righteousness; the second half honours his goodness and trustworthiness. Psalm 112 first describes the happy condition of those who allow God to work in their lives, its second half, our position of trust in God.

Frank Ballard writes:

This then is the good life as it is sketched by the Hebrew poet. It is not a finished portrait. Nor is it a perfect picture. For perfection, let it be said again, we must pass beyond O.T. pages to the strong Son of God, who gave his life a ransom for many. There we find forgiveness without self-righteousness, mercy and magnanimity without condescension or condoning; love that knew no limits, yet never descended to sentimentality.[24]

Psalm 111 ends with the reminder that wisdom begins with the fear of the Lord. Then Psalm 112 opens by continuing the thought that those who fear the Lord are truly happy and delight in his Word. We rejoice that God crowns such followers with enduring blessing.

I Witness

'I have seen and I testify that this is the Son of God' (v. 34).

After eighteen verses of prologue, John begins his narrative. Jewish leaders in Jerusalem, some of those who reject Jesus, send a deputation of officials to John the Baptist to confront him. These priests could have particular interest in the baptiser since he is the son of a priest. Besides, he has a peculiar ministry and attracts crowds. Is he the Messiah?

In the first of his several uses of the emphatic *I*, the baptiser is definite. His mode of response indicates that although he is not the Messiah, the Messiah *is* here. The delegation relentlessly continues – are you Elijah or the prophet? (These were both preparatory figures the Jews anticipated to herald the Messiah.) To these John curtly replies, 'I am not' and 'no'.

Exasperated and needing an answer for their leaders, they ask him: 'Who are you?' The other three Gospels refer to John as the 'voice in the wilderness' (Isaiah 40:3), but in this Gospel John records the baptiser answering with that quotation himself. He piques their curiosity. If he's not the Christ, Elijah or the prophet, why is he baptising so liberally? Unauthorised, he has no right to the rite.

John simply points to one who comes after him who is far worthier than he. The next day he sees Jesus coming and identifies him as that worthier one, the Lamb of God, the world's sin-bearer. His testimony is specific. This is the one he saw the Spirit perch on, as God had said would happen. He is the Son of God.

Jesus comes! Let all adore him!
Lord of mercy, love and truth.
Now prepare the way before him,
Make the rugged places smooth;
Through the desert mark his road,
Make a highway for our God.
Thomas Kelly (*SASB* 159)

Receivers

'The first thing Andrew did was to find his brother Simon and tell him,
"We have found the Messiah" (that is, the Christ). And he brought
him to Jesus' (vv. 41, 42).

John now identifies some of those 'who received him' (v. 12). Several
become Christ's disciples: Andrew, Peter, Philip, Nathaniel and,
although unnamed, John. Here as elsewhere John is reluctant to name
himself, but is doubtless one of the baptiser's two disciples who turn to
follow Jesus, perhaps at a distance, until he asks them what they seek (vv.
35–38). Jesus invites them to come with him. They spend the rest of the
day in his company.

Another phrase in verse 12 – 'the right to become' – ties in with some of
Christ's exchanges with these earliest disciples. The Greek word for 'right'
here is *exousia*. This is not just the possibility of becoming, but the
authorisation and power to become.

We think about that when Jesus tells Simon he will become Peter
(a rock) and when he tells Nathaniel he'll see greater things. Jesus would
enable them both. Doesn't he do the same for any who believe in him?
Jesus not only sees us as we are and gives us vision for something more,
but enables us to become what *The Message* calls our true 'child-of-God
selves' (v. 12).

In this initial chapter alone John uses a number of descriptive titles for
the Lord: living Word; Light, sacrificial Lamb of God; Son of God; Rabbi,
master teacher; Messiah, the Christ; the God-man Jesus of Nazareth; King
of Israel; and Son of man. Some primarily show his relationship with the
Father; others primarily demonstrate his function towards humankind. All
are interrelated and significant.

Besides John's emphases on concepts such as 'receive' and 'right to
become', descriptive titles of Christ introduced in chapter 1 will also recur
and be developed throughout the book.

If we ask the Holy Spirit to speak to us through the Word and are alert
receivers, willing to obey what he says, God will emphasise what we need
to hear and enable us to apply it for his glory. Amen.

Wedding Grace

'He thus revealed his glory and his disciples put their faith in him' (v. 11).

The first of the eight specially selected miracles John relates takes place at an actual wedding. In his teaching Jesus will frequently use wedding metaphors for the kingdom of heaven. Whose wedding does Jesus attend in Cana, Galilee? Some scholars suggest it could have been John's. They point out that it is recorded only in John's Gospel and that it has the detail of an eye-witness. John may have been related to Jesus. That would explain why Jesus and his mother were invited and why she was concerned for the family about the shortage of wine.

Even at this early stage in Jesus' ministry, Mary must know him well enough to realise that he cares about human need and that she can trust him. In a lovely simplicity we can emulate, she instinctively turns to Jesus and tells him the problem.

What in older versions may sound like Jesus rebuffing Mary, 'What have I to do with thee?' (v. 4, *KJV*), may be better represented: 'Leave it to me.' And the older versions' address of 'woman' should more accurately be rendered to reflect the more respectful and affectionate address it is, such as 'dear woman' or 'my lady'. It is the same term Jesus uses when he addresses Mary from the cross and entrusts her to John's care (19:26).

Mary's confident instruction to the servants to do whatever Jesus tells them may reassure them that a solution is possible even with only what is to hand. Possibly for the sake of his Gentile readers, John details the stone water pots and their usual Jewish function.

Jesus gives clear instructions: fill the pots with water. The servants comply completely – filling them to the brim. We don't know when the water is transformed, but by the time they obediently draw some out and take it to the one in charge, it tastes like choice wine.

Inadequate resources become abundance. Disappointment becomes joy. When Jesus kindly intervenes and saves a family from humiliation he reveals his glory. The disciples notice and put their faith in him. Where do we glimpse Christ's grace and glory today?

Temple Refiner

*'After he was raised from the dead . . . then they believed the Scripture
and the words that Jesus had spoken' (v. 22).*

The other Gospels place Jesus cleansing the temple on Monday of Holy
Week near the close of his ministry. John does not write a chronological
biography. John's record of the incident places it just before Passover and
may well be the same event the other Gospel writers describe. He does not
assemble his particular facts for a timeline but to portray the truth that
Jesus is the Son of God.

William Barclay suggests that John probably recalls the prophecies of
the coming Messiah, such as Malachi 3:1–4, which speak of the Lord,
white-hot as from a smelter's furnace, suddenly coming to his temple to
cleanse and refine the priests until they're fit to present offerings of righteousness. When John writes that Jesus cleanses the temple, he proclaims in
another way that Jesus is that long-promised Messiah.

Temple offerings needed to be made in temple currency, so initially a
money-changing service could have been helpful. But most money-
changers and those who sold animals for sacrifices found ways to exploit
the pilgrims who travelled to Jerusalem. As is usually the case, the poorest
were affected most.

Theoretically, animals could be purchased elsewhere at reasonable
prices and then nominally taxed at the temple. But animal vendors
colluded with inspectors so that the animals brought to the temple from
elsewhere would be rejected and the people would have to pay prices they
could not afford to buy temple-sanctioned animals. Underlying avarice
desecrated God's house.

John records two reactions of bystanders when Jesus upended the coin
tables and chased the animals out of the temple. The disciples remember
words from Psalm 69:9 about being consumed with zeal for God's house.
Conversely, the Jewish leadership ask Jesus for a sign to justify his authority
for such rash action. His answer and its allusion to his resurrection will
finally make sense to some, but only after Easter. Christ's victory helps us
trust his purposes.

Born from Above

*'Unless a person is born from above, it's not possible to see what
I'm pointing to – to God's kingdom' (v. 3, MSG).*

The final verses of chapter 2 are a transition into chapter 3. We don't
know what miracles Jesus performs while in Jerusalem, but they appeal
to many people there enough to stir a measure of faith in him and the
notion he might possibly be the Messiah.

But Jesus knows better than to trust himself to people of superficial faith
whose hearts haven't turned to him. He has keen discernment of human
nature and is cognisant of each person's heart condition. John wants
readers to realise that when Jesus confronts a person, their deepest needs
and sins are exposed. John goes on to give a prime example of Jesus'
penetrating knowledge of people's hearts.

Nicodemus is probably wealthy. Later he will bring a costly seventy-five
pounds of myrrh and aloes to embalm Christ's body (John 19:39). He is a
Pharisee, a separated religious man, one of a select Jewish brotherhood
pledged for life to abide by the law of Moses and its addendum of scribal
law's ins and outs. He is devout and earnest about pleasing God by obeying
all the rules.

He is likely a member of the seventy-member Sanhedrin Supreme
Court. With such a standing, it is astonishing that he seeks out Jesus at all.
Night-time allows him to cautiously and privately come to Jesus for an
interview. He addresses Christ as 'rabbi' or teacher and refers to his recent
miracles that show he must enjoy God's special favour. Jesus replies that
only those born from above can see God's kingdom – that absolute
dominion of God which the Jews anticipated would be fully realised with
the Messiah's coming.

If Nicodemus could take what Jesus says as confirmation of his
observations of God's blessing on Jesus' ministry, Jesus' reply might
encourage him. But Jesus' reply catches him off guard. The scholar latches
onto 'birth' and says it is incongruous with old age. Jesus tries to raise the
seeker's sights to things of the Spirit, things that are above, with images of
the cleansing and refreshing traits of water and wind. What is the Lord
using to raise our sights?

'We'

'We speak of what we know, and we testify to what we have seen' (v. 11).

The way Jesus interacts with Nicodemus is typical of his encounters with other enquirers. Jesus counters simple statements or questions with replies that may at first sometimes be difficult to grasp yet intrigue the enquirer. They may make the seeker think deeply about important spiritual issues. Jesus tailors the conversation to the person's life and its core issues.

Quite possibly Nicodemus yearns for the 'born from above' experience Jesus claims is necessary, but doesn't see that it is possible. Nicodemus asks, 'How can this be?' (v. 9) from his awareness that no amount of study or self-discipline has accomplished such a transformation in his life.

His question isn't exactly the 'how' Zechariah raised when the angel told him his elderly wife would have a child. That was more of a request for proof. Nicodemus doesn't ask in the tenor of Mary's question at the annunciation. She accepted her appointment of Christ-bearer, but wondered how she'd become pregnant.

Being born again was a familiar concept. Jews of the day spoke of converts to Judaism as being reborn and signified conversions with baptisms. Greek mystery religions initiated converts with rites and called them twice-borns. The concept of rebirth (new life, regeneration, re-creation) continues throughout the New Testament. For Christians, rebirth is interwoven with entering the kingdom of heaven, the family of God and eternal life. In chapter 3 it is associated with the 'kingdom of God' (vv. 3, 5).

Such rebirth requires our obedience to God's will in cooperation with his saving grace. That experience of believers through the centuries is succinctly stated in a doctrine of Christian faith as taught in The Salvation Army: 'We believe that repentance towards God, faith in our Lord Jesus Christ, and regeneration by the Holy Spirit, are necessary to salvation.'

Isn't it likely that the 'we' in verse 11 who speak, know, testify and see includes all those reborn by the Spirit and following Christ?

The Eternally Perfect One

'Such a high priest meets our need – one who is holy, blameless, pure, set apart from sinners, exalted above the heavens' (Hebrews 7:26).

A Jewish commentary says that because of Psalm 110:4's reference to the king being a priest after the manner of Melchizedek, the whole psalm, written by David, has received many interpretations. Some say it refers to Abraham who met Melchizedek (Genesis 14:18). Most Jewish commentators say that the psalm refers to King David. Some allow it may relate to one of David's successors.

It obviously speaks of royalty and asks God's blessing on his anointed one. In that way it is similar to Psalms 20, 21 and 45. The king described in Psalm 110 is David's Lord.

In the first verse, The Lord (*Yahweh* – Eternal One) tells the Lord (*Adonai*) to sit at his right hand. Who sits at the right hand of God but the Messiah? Jesus referred to this verse in speaking of himself (Mark 12:35–37) and the Jewish leaders he addressed understood what he meant. It is quoted twenty other times in the New Testament, each time referring to Christ and his kingdom. It is clearly a Messianic psalm.

The psalmist says the one extolled is a priest for ever in the order of Melchizedek, the King of Salem (or peace). Melchizedek predated the Levitical order and the law and was without ancestry. He was not a priest of a nation, but of the Most High God. Hebrews 7, a good companion to this psalm, tells us that Melchizedek's name means king of righteousness. That priest–king was an early type of Christ – our Prince of Peace, King of Righteousness and everlasting Priest of God.

Jesus, the holy, undefiled, sinless, perfect one gave his life for us once for all. Hallelujah!

Thine is the glory,
Risen, conquering Son;
Endless is the victory
Thou o'er death hast won.
    Edmond Louis Budry, trs. Richard Birch Hoyle
    (*SASB* 152)

Into the Light

'But those who live by the truth come into the light, so that it
may be seen plainly that what they have done has been done
in the sight of God' (v. 21, TNIV).

Jesus turns the conversation to concrete particulars. After he refers to himself as the one who came from heaven, he introduces something from the time when the chosen people wandered in the wilderness. More than once during that period they had to learn first-hand that the only remedy for their costly disobedience was a radical repentance and return to God on his terms.

Nicodemus would know the story of the people who unjustifiably speak against God and Moses until they're punished by a plague of snakes. They repent and, in answer to Moses' prayer for them, God gives a unique remedy raised high enough to be seen by anyone (see Numbers 21:4–9). Jesus says he himself would similarly be lifted up and the lives of those who believe in him saved.

The root of the word John uses for lifted up has two connotations. One is of something physically elevated and able to be seen, such as a hoisted flag. The other is of someone who is exalted. So John characteristically blends Christ's cross and glory. The well-known and loved words of John 3:16 fittingly follow. Although many of us have favourite Bible verses, this one is said to be 'everybody's text'.

So why, after a declaration of God's great initiative of love, must thoughts of judgment and darkness meet us in subsequent verses? In his usual straightforward way of speaking, Jesus plainly states that people are free to accept or refuse the gift God offers. Unbelief and faith both have natural long-term and short-term consequences: darkness and condemnation or light and life.

Ironically, Jesus finishes this night-time interview with Nicodemus with references to light (vv. 19–21). Perhaps he wants to challenge a secret seeker to open allegiance. Later Nicodemus does speak up to the Pharisees on Jesus' behalf. Later he and another dare to approach Pilate to request Jesus' body and prepare it for respectful burial. They came into the light as Jesus hoped they would.

Second Fiddlers Wanted

'He must grow greater and greater and I less and less' (v. 30, JBP).

Jesus moves away from Jerusalem and into the neighbouring Judean countryside to spend some time with his disciples. At a nearby abundant water source John the Baptist continues to welcome those who want to be baptised. Meanwhile other seekers start to gravitate to Jesus and his disciples for the same purpose.

An argument emerges between John's followers and some of the Jews about purification. Some still consider baptism to be ceremonial washing while others like John see it as signalling a change of direction, a promise to hear and obey God and be ready for the Messiah. Baptism cannot take away a person's sins. Only God can do that.

But the core of the controversy is likely whether being baptised by Jesus or John is more effective and preferable. John knows they want him to corroborate their resentment of Jesus. Instead he stays poised and gently reminds them that under God's sovereignty we all have a role to fill (v. 27). He restates what he said before, that he is not the Christ, but is his herald (v. 28).

He compares their relationship to that of a bridegroom and his best man (v. 29). Because of who the bridegroom is, rather than feeling upstaged, the friend is completely delighted for him to be the focal point and says: 'This is the assigned moment for him to move into the center, while I slip off to the sidelines' (v. 30, *MSG*).

In the Franco-centric cycling world, when someone who is capable of being out in front is willing to take second place to enable another to win, they say he takes *domestique* (servant) status. Where the *domestique* finishes in a race is less important than the help he gives. Solo horn players or violinists value those whose parts are rarely featured, but provide consistent support. People who recognise they can do their best work in subordinate roles and do it willingly and well are rare treasures. The apostle Paul knew many and gladly recognised them (see Romans 16). More importantly, the Lord notices and rewards the players of small parts.

First-Hand Knowledge

'He is sent by God. He speaks God's words, for God gives
him the Spirit without limit. Anyone who believes in God's Son
has eternal life' (vv. 34, 36, NLT).

Some scholars include the final six verses of chapter 3 as a continuation of what John the Baptist was saying. However, most hold that these verses are John the writer's words about Christ and are suitably placed to follow the baptiser's declaration. The first sentence speaks of the one from heaven and the one from earth – no doubt referring to Jesus and John: 'The earthborn is earthbound and speaks earth language; the heavenborn is in a league of his own' (v. 31, *MSG*).

John describes Jesus, the one who comes from above and is supreme, as the witness about heaven and God. He tells us what he has seen and heard. His is the ultimate primary source. Only Jesus fully knows God, so he's the only one qualified to give us first-hand knowledge.

John says that although Christ's witness is rejected by many, those who receive it do so wholeheartedly by attesting to its truth as if signing their names to a binding document. 'He who has received his testimony has set his seal to *this*, that God is true' (v. 33, *NASB*).

The One God sent, the living Word, speaks the word of God (the full message) by the limitless Spirit of God. So listening to Jesus is hearing God's voice. Further, the Father gives the One he loves total responsibility for humankind's redemption (v. 35). Jesus is God's plan 'A' for the human race and there is no plan 'B'.

Therefore faith in Christ issues in eternal life. It is a present reality (note the present tense of the verb 'has' in v. 36) with continuous benefits and future implications. The alternative to faith in Christ is disbelief, neglect or refusal to obey him. It too has consequences. As one commentator advises us, it is a kindness that Christ 'will make no compromise with us, but demands obedience, here and now on pain of parting with him'.[25] God's strong love is true to his nature and his word. Our heart's response is crucial.

Straight Way

'Give me this water! Then I'll never be thirsty again' (v. 15, NLT).

Our family once lived on a street which, although somewhat curved, connected two of the town's main arteries. It was called Straightway. When Jesus and his disciples leave the mistaken rivalry over baptism and head for Galilee, they take the less travelled but most direct route which crosses Samaria. As it happens, it takes more time than expected.

While Jesus rests near a well in an historic area, the disciples go into the town for food. Their willingness to intentionally enter a Samaritan town and encounter the locals is telling. Most Jews would rather go hungry than deal with the hated Samaritans. Has their time with Jesus begun to give them a new perspective?

Trouble started more than seven centuries earlier when conquering armies deported most of the Jews in the northern kingdom and brought in other people groups to settle and hold the region. The Jews who remained married the foreigners and lost their racial purity. But when the Jews of the south were exiled, they remained pure, so felt superior to the Samaritans and despised them for their compromise. They even refused their northern neighbours' help in rebuilding the temple around 450 BC.

The bitterness festered and continued to Jesus' day. It's no wonder that the woman who comes for water is suspicious of a Jewish man who speaks to her even though it seems to be without disdain.

The form of the conversation sounds familiar. Jesus says something figurative that is taken literally and misunderstood. Jesus patiently furthers the dialogue until inquirers finally face themselves and recognise their true need. Here Jesus offers the woman what everyone needs most – the living water of eternal life.

The old way is symbolised by water, the new by the fulfilment Jesus brings to life. Recall from earlier chapters the six water pots and serving the best wine last, born of water and born of the Spirit. Now it's Jacob's well water and water springing up to everlasting life. Hallelujah for Christ's refreshing new way!

Relieved and Refreshed

'Then Jesus told her, "I AM the Messiah!"' (v. 26, NLT).

Does changing the subject from living water to 'go get your husband' seem strange? Jesus makes the appeal to the unnamed woman of Sychar to reach her at another level.

He appealed to her kindness when he requested a drink. He appealed to her curiosity when he said if she'd realised who he was she could have asked him for water. He appealed to her soul-thirst when he talked about living water. Now he touches on her life worn out by sin. His reply to her initial denial of having a husband only draws her closer.

How could he know? Practised in flattery, she compliments him as a prophet; then cleverly diverts the topic to a safer matter than sin, a religious one within the province of a prophet. Instead of something so uncomfortably close to truth about her heart, she turns to a longstanding religious issue. Her people traditionally worship at a mountain within sight of Sychar (Gerizim), while the Jews insist on Jerusalem.

What does Jesus think? He isn't deterred by her tactic, but goes beyond her question of tradition and location and appeals to her sense of God. It's worship from one's heart that counts most, as long as it is in spirit and truth. She has nowhere to hide. She turns to the one thing besides early patriarchal history the Samaritans and Jews still hold in common: anticipation of the Messiah who will make everything plain.

Finally Jesus appeals to her hope. What Jesus hasn't said to the Jews because they expect the Messiah to come with a zealous political agenda, he can plainly tell a Samaritan woman without being misunderstood: 'I am that Messiah.' Now she is face to face with Truth. What a blessed relief.

The Lord lovingly appeals to each of us, first to bring us into faith and then to help us to grow in Christian faith. If we respond to the truth he speaks to our hearts, we too will be relieved and refreshed.

See and Seize

'And because of his words many more became believers' (v. 41).

The conversation is ended, but for the woman, new life has just begun. The disciples return and are surprised at what they see. At this point they don't know anything about her background, so that can't be the cause of their amazement. They themselves have just been to town and bought food from Samaritans, so his interacting with a Samaritan isn't what surprises them.

Their master is talking with a woman in public. Jewish men don't talk with women in the street. It could cause gossip. It is considered a waste of time for a rabbi to teach a woman. Some Jews don't even look at women in public. Those who carry this to extremes and shield their eyes are sometimes known as 'the bruised ones' because they tend to bump into things.

The woman of Sychar, Samaria, doesn't wait to chat with the disciples. She is so dumbfounded at meeting one who acts as if he is the Messiah that she leaves her still dry, empty water pot and heads for town. She'll be back. Her extra midday trek for water is now nothing compared with her overflowing news. She is so sure of Jesus that with a full heart she runs to encounter people she normally avoids or who might normally shun her.

When his disciples left Jesus at the well he was weary. Now he seems energised. When they urge him to eat he uses the opportunity to tell them what really satisfies him is doing God's will and accomplishing his mission of transforming lives. He sees people with diseased hearts, but knows what their healthy hearts will look like when restored. He urges the disciples to see and seize every opportunity to spread the good news of the kingdom of God.

The woman who has religious head knowledge but doesn't see its relevance to her life has a spiritual 'aha' moment with Jesus and she's on the road to heart health. This is too good to keep secret, so she tells others. In just two days many of Sychar have spiritual heart transplants and miraculously believe for themselves that this Jew, Jesus, is the Saviour of the world, even for Samaritans (v. 42).

Palm Sunday – Passion Sunday

*'My mouth's full of great praise for GOD, I'm singing his hallelujahs
surrounded by crowds' (v. 30, MSG).*

I t is thought that David was the likely composer of nearly half the psalms.
He wrote perhaps 20 per cent of those when he experienced deep
trouble. In all but one of these written from the springboard of a negative
situation, David ends up praising the Lord. Is he a Pollyanna of Israel? Not
really. He is able to express his anguish to God, call on his help and rest
assured that the Lord will not fail him. There is a balance of trouble and
triumph.

Likewise there is something of the bitter sweet on this sixth Sunday of
Lent when Christians observe the triumphal entry of Jesus into Jerusalem.
John 12 tells us that many of the crowd who are in Jerusalem for Passover
come out to greet him exuberantly because they heard he'd raised Lazarus
from the dead.

Jesus is not swayed from his mission even when he seems so popular
that in dismay the Pharisees say the whole world is running after him.
Within the week the crowd's rising acceptance of him will collapse like an
under-baked soufflé.

Instead of basking in popular praise, Jesus speaks of losing his life. Yet
Jesus does not allow the cross before him to keep him from encouraging
others to faithfulness. He urges his followers to imitate him in sacrificial
living (John 12:23–25).

Jesus admits that his soul is troubled at the prospect of his violent death,
but knows this is his appointment. He doesn't recoil from doing God's will,
but at the suffering that obedience will cost. So instead of asking for
deliverance, he asks that God's name be glorified. As happened at Jesus'
baptism and transfiguration, a voice thunders from heaven to testify of
Jesus' divine mission and assure him of the coming ultimate divine victory
(John 12:28).

Many churches refer to this first day of Holy Week, Palm Sunday, as
Passion Sunday and incorporate some emphasis on the start of Christ's
final journey to Calvary in their worship. On this Lord's Day we praise
God while mindful of the great cost of our salvation.

Clean Feet and Humble Hearts

'Jesus knew that the time had come for him to leave this world and go to the Father. Having loved his own who were in the world, he now showed them the full extent of his love' (v. 1).

This year the Jewish Passover begins tonight at sundown. On the day that it's celebrated in Jesus' last week, Thursday, Luke's Gospel tells us Jesus sends John and Peter to arrange for their Passover evening meal. A few days earlier Jesus was honoured at the home of Mary, Martha and Lazarus. The memory of the meal, conversation, fragrant foot-washing, criticism, curious crowds and undercurrent of indignant Jewish leadership lingers (12:1–8).

Throughout his ministry Jesus repeatedly refers to 'his hour'. In some cases he means the time of his being recognised as the Messiah. Other times he means the time of his crucifixion. All through his life Jesus is aware that he moves towards fulfilling God's primary purpose for him. After repeatedly saying his hour had not yet come, this week Jesus says it's time: 'Time's up. The time has come for the Son of Man to be glorified' (12:23, *MSG*).

The cross is imminent. Events gain momentum and import. We don't know what the other disciples think when Jesus washes their feet at the Last Supper, but Scripture tells us that when he reaches Peter, the outspoken disciple objects. Does he oppose his master taking the role of a servant? Does he remember Mary's sacrificial act and seek to keep Jesus from taking such a role with him?

After a brief word from Jesus, Peter wants a full bath. There is nothing half-hearted about this follower. Jesus assures him that this simply is the time for clean feet, then goes on to explain the significance of what he has done.

Being his follower isn't a matter of a show of hands, but of humble actions. His loving, servant leadership needs to continue through them. Hereafter clean feet will remind them of his lesson. In a few minutes he says it outright: 'In the same way I loved you, you love one another' (13:34, *MSG*). How can we follow his command today?

At a Distance

'I have told you these things so that you won't abandon your faith'
(John 16:1, NLT).

As soon as Judas leaves the Last Supper, Jesus again says 'the time has come' and proceeds to tell the disciples that he will be leaving them shortly. Peter insists he would die for Jesus, but Jesus knows him well and interrupts his bravado: You'll die for me? No, by morning you'll deny me (John 13:37, 38).

John records the assuring words and instructions Jesus gives his followers as through metaphor and plain speech he comforts them, reminds them of their vital union with him and promises that the Holy Spirit will come to them. He's realistic about troubles that will come, but also talks about a coming joy that's worth the trouble. At last they affirm their faith in him.

John does not record Jesus' struggle in prayer in the Garden of Gethsemane or the failure of the disciples to watch and pray with him. However, John alone records the beautiful prayer Jesus prays for his followers before leaving the upper room. It is the ultimate and timeless benediction applicable to all followers of Christ.

By the time Judas brings a cadre of soldiers and officials to the garden to arrest Jesus, Peter's mind isn't on what Jesus said or prayed. In the blaze of torches, Peter overreacts with a sword as he tries to keep the Master from his painful mission (John 18:10, 11).

John tells us Peter and another disciple follow Jesus to the high priest's court. All four Gospels record Peter's presence in the courtyard. Three say Peter followed at a distance. At that point, how true that is, not only spatially but also spiritually.

In the blaze of the courtyard fire the erstwhile brazen follower, now on his own, cowers and denies Christ three times. The rooster crows. Jesus looks at Peter. When that sound and look sear the truth of what Peter has done onto his soul, he weeps with remorse (Luke 22:61, 62). This Holy Week may be the fitting time to examine our motives, commitments and dedication to Christ. Is there anything keeping us at a distance from the Master?

There's More

*'They still did not understand from Scripture that Jesus had
to rise from the dead' (v. 9).*

When Judas hears that the chief priests and elders have condemned Jesus to death, he tries to return the money he's received for betraying Christ. He flings it into the temple and leaves to hang himself in despair.

We don't have any record of what Peter does after his bitter experience of disowning Christ, but he definitely doesn't follow Judas's path to suicide. Does Peter slink about in the darkness furtively waiting to hear what happens to Jesus when he's falsely accused by Jewish religious leaders, interrogated by Pilate and Herod, scourged by soldiers?

Since Mark's Gospel is thought to be based on Peter's accounts, what Peter observes from the sidelines on Friday is probably in Mark 15. If so, although not named, Peter is in the vicinity of the cross when Jesus dies and when Joseph of Arimathea takes Christ's body away for burial.

How telling that when the women encounter the angel on Easter morning, the angel's message to them is that Jesus is risen and they should tell his disciples *and Peter* (Mark 16:7). Mary runs to Peter and John with news that Jesus' body is missing. Peter doesn't need to think twice.

The two men race for the tomb. John and Luke both tell us that the men see the empty grave clothes and then go home (John 20:6, 7; Luke 22:12). Whereas most of the disciples are dubious about the women's report of angels and their talk of a risen Jesus, John adds that he, 'the other disciple', sees and believes. Luke adds that Peter marvels at what has happened.

Perhaps Peter's hope is growing that his failure to stay awake and pray with Jesus in Gethsemane, his hasty use of a sword, his triple denial in the courtyard, Christ's silent look as he passed him, and even the horror of the cross aren't the end of the story. He'll soon learn there is so much more. Indeed, so do we all.

Recommissioned

'He said, "Lord, you know everything. You know that I love you."
Jesus said, "Then feed my sheep"' (v. 17, NLT).

Jesus knew he had to finish the work his Father gave him to do and said so more than once. He lived his whole life with a unique purpose that gave him direction. All of sacred history pointed towards his culminating sacrifice. We sense that his teaching and actions intensify as he approaches the cross.

If you knew you had only a week to live, how would you spend your final days? Right up until the last twenty-four hours of the week when his betrayal, mock trial, scourging, sentencing and crucifixion take precedence, Jesus chooses to spend time with those in whom he's invested so much.

It takes his followers some time and several encounters with the risen Christ to begin to understand how much he has accomplished by his life, death and resurrection. First they start to understand it individually and personally. For forty days people meet him: the women, Peter, two on the Emmaus road, eleven disciples, James, seven disciples and eventually more than 500 see him and can verify he really is alive.

Whatever else Jesus plans to accomplish in the meeting, when Peter and six others discover Jesus on the lakeshore in Galilee one morning, Peter seems singled out for attention. Perhaps he represents all of us in some way. Jesus doesn't ask Peter for a fresh repentance of his failure; he knows his earlier repentance and remorse were sincere and deep.

Jesus may want to spare Peter from further despair. He gives Peter opportunity to declare that he loves his Master supremely. When he owns that he truly loves the Lord, he receives a task of service. Love involves responsibility and sacrifice. It was so for Jesus and would be for his followers until Christ's mission is accomplished.

When we confess our love for Christ, what does he ask of us? Recognising the brevity of life adds urgency and encourages us to be purposeful, commissioned Christians.

He Has Done It!

'Posterity will serve him; future generations will be told about the LORD.
They will proclaim his righteousness to a people yet unborn –
for he has done it' (vv. 30, 31).

Salvationist Peter M. Cooke's poem 'Out of the Depths'[26] and Psalm 22,
which many commentators hold as written about the cross, help us
today to meditate on the scope of the price of Jesus' sacrifice for us.

> A darkness thick and deep as moss,
> A gloom no lightning can descry
> Surrounds a hillside and a cross
> Where hangs the world's true Light to die.
>
> The parched earth pants with heaviest thirst,
> No flowers grow, nor friendly trees.
> The throbbing mound it seems must burst
> For lack of streams or cooling breeze.
>
> No grateful music echoes here,
> No hum of bee, nor song of bird.
> The wind's dull moan has ceased to sear
> The hearer's ear, no more is heard.
>
> A mother's sob, a friend's soft moan,
> A stream of blood, a flashing spear,
> The temple vein it seems is torn,
> The day-dawn breaks, new light is here.
>
> Now is fulfilled the prophet's song:
> 'They look upon him whom they pierced'.
> Light, love and life to him belong,
> Blessing is theirs who once were cursed.

Finishing Grace in the Shadow of Death

'Even though I walk through the valley of the shadow of death,
I will fear no evil, for you are with me; your rod and your staff,
they comfort me' (v. 4).

In winter before I walk along the wooded trail that skirts the Hudson River, I consider the time of day. The cliffs that run along the west side of the trail block the sunlight and overshadow the woods earlier than I would expect.

The day between Good Friday and Easter is overshadowed by death. The first followers of Jesus don't realise what he means when he says from the cross, *tetelestai*, 'It is finished' (John 19:30). They think their lives and dreams are dead along with their Master. They don't know that in Christ's sacrificial death, everything in sacred history that had been unfinished, every symbol that had pointed to this time is now perfectly complete.

To the devil and his horde it means certain doom. To the angels, patriarchs and prophets cheering from heaven, it means absolute victory. What Christ's sacrifice on the cross perfectly accomplished has continuing effect.

Some churches hold *tenebrae* (shadows) services on Thursday, Friday or Saturday of Holy Week. During a series of Scripture readings gradually the lights are extinguished until all is dark. It symbolises the darkness at Jesus' death and the hopelessness of a world without God. The worshippers leave in silence to wait.

Jesus experienced the anguish of death by crucifixion for us. Because of Christ's death, when we trust him our own death, as unwelcome and dreadful as the prospect may be, is a shadow without a sting. The psalmist says that even in the shadow of the valley of death he will not fear evil because the Lord is with him.

The Message says: 'In the resurrection scheme of things . . . now in a single victorious stroke of Life, all three – sin, guilt, death – are gone, the gift of our Master, Jesus Christ. Thank God!' (1 Corinthians 15:53, 57). He is with us. We can trust him now and for his finishing grace.

Christ is the King of Glory

*'Who is this King of glory? The LORD of hosts, He is the
King of glory' (v. 10, NKJV).*

Today's psalm speaks of the resurrection. The conquering Christ is victorious over Satan and death. He is the Lord of hosts, mighty in battle. He is the King of glory. After the focus on Jesus' broken body, Easter is a relief. In dramatic contrast with Good Friday's sombreness, we enjoy Easter's flowers and stirring music.

But the Risen Lord doesn't stay in the garden. Even on the first Easter Day he appears to his followers in everyday situations of walks and meals and allows them to look at him, to touch him, to raise questions. Rather than diverting their eyes from his wounds, he invites their touch. Rather than avoiding their puzzlement, he carefully explains what the Scripture says about him.

Jesus still comes to meet us in our everyday round and opens our understanding. He makes us more than conquerors. Praise him!

> Lo! Jesus meets thee,
> Risen from the tomb;
> Lovingly he greets thee,
> Scatters fear and gloom;
> Let his Church with gladness
> Hymns of triumph sing,
> For her Lord now liveth;
> Death has lost its sting.
>
> No more we doubt thee,
> Glorious Prince of Life!
> Life is naught without thee;
> Aid us in thy strife;
> Make us more than conquerors
> Through thy deathless love;
> Bring us safe through Jordan
> To thy home above.
>
> *Edmond Louis Budry* trs. Richard Birch Hoyle
> (*SASB* 152)

Intimacy of Wounds

*'Put your hand into the wound in my side. Don't be faithless
any longer. Believe!' (v. 27, NLT).*

In some places Easter lasts two days and today is celebrated as Easter
Monday. In other traditions Easter Monday is the second day of Easter
Week or Bright Week. The first disciples' continued encounters with Christ
after his resurrection must bolster their faith and joy. For all believers
Easter joy certainly spills over beyond a single day or season.

Initially Christ's disciples stay to themselves, closeted away as if hiding
in a tomb of their own. The second time Jesus appears to the group,
Thomas is there. Jesus invites the disciples to look at his wounds. Easter
comes as a great relief and we move away from the physicality of Good
Friday. Other than for medical help, we usually don't invite scrutiny of any
of our wounds or stare at those of others. But Jesus enters their everyday
world and invites his followers to just such an intimacy.

Jesus was not born wounded, but chose to be wounded for us. When he
exposes those wounds to his disciples, he comes with a greeting of whole-
ness and peace, *Shalom Aleichem* – 'Peace be with you' (John 20:26). His
wounds bring us true peace (Isaiah 53:5). He who knows suffering
intimately can be trusted when he offers us real peace in our woundedness.
Through Christ we can join his company of wounded healers.

After his resurrection, although in a body suited for heaven and capable
of passing through locked doors, Jesus is down to earth – breaking bread,
eating fish, bread and honey, cooking, explaining Scripture, affirming his
followers and challenging them to wait for divine empowerment and then
a widespread witness for him.

To ponder:

'If we truly seek Jesus, he will come. For, he wants always to do a greater work in
us. And if we long for this, he will come and do it.'

Commissioner Maxwell Feener (in his online devotional thoughts
Comm. Cast, 15 March 2010)

In Quietness and Confidence

Introduction

Some people thrive on social interaction. Others need solitude. After an extended period of hosting visitors in her small retirement home a gentle, contemplative friend admitted: 'I'm not good when people crowd in on my space so I have been doing a fair bit of apologising and repenting!' While some temperaments require more of one or the other, most of us try to balance times of social activity and quiet seclusion.

We know that even though Jesus is constantly in demand by people with all types of needs, he carves out time to meet privately with his disciples and instruct them. Yet he also requires the solitude of prayer. Often Jesus finds his circle of quiet on a mountain (Mark 1:35). On the night he is arrested, he prays in an olive grove (Mark 14:32). Since he intentionally sought a quiet place to meet with God, shouldn't we as well?

The Christian calendar sometimes helps. Christmas celebrations follow Advent preparations. Easter follows Lenten contemplation. But after the festive days we may sense a need for time to reflect on recent joys. For a few post-Easter days let us consider the help that quietness can bring to our spirits as we seek to be still in God's presence.

Circle of Quiet

'Jesus came, took the bread and gave it to them, and did the
same with the fish' (v. 13).

After Easter, when Peter and his friends go fishing in Galilee, it may be in part for the respite they'd known at the lake. Some people know where to find their circle of quiet. In her book, *A Circle of Quiet*, Madeleine L'Engle describes needing to find hers one summer when a dozen or so from the four generations of her family shared an old farmhouse: 'My special place is a small brook in a green glade, a circle of quiet from which there is no visible sign of human beings . . . [there] I move slowly into a kind of peace that is indeed marvellous.'[27]

A Christian retreat centre on New York's Hudson River hosts a conference for those who seek God, but feel brain-weary from being bombarded by society's countless verbal and written messages. Even those who work with words for a living need a break from the barrage of words. The beauty of creation, art or music can help. While living within a few miles of that river, my husband and I have delighted in walking the river's quiet, wooded, west-bank trails in all seasons. At times we've sat at the river's edge to think and pray. It's been a personal mini-retreat and balm for us.

We visited the river before supper early one spring. The region had recently experienced strong storms that toppled trees and left many homes without power. The devastation capped a particularly harsh winter. The mounds of driftwood thrown up on the rocky shore testified to the river's recent turbulence. But that evening the river was placid, without a ripple. The visual calm and silence were palpable. It was like the relief a day of azure skies and freshly scrubbed air brings after a typhoon or hurricane.

After the crash of Good Friday and upsurge of Easter, when the disciples unexpectedly meet the Risen Christ on the shore, he knows the flotsam in their lives and offers them food and companionship in a circle of quiet. After they've eaten he begins the dialogue towards restoration. Are we meeting him in these post-Easter days?

In Quietness

'God, the Master, the Holy of Israel, has this solemn counsel:
"Your salvation requires you to turn back to me and stop your silly
efforts to save yourselves. Your strength will come from settling down
in complete dependence on me"' (v. 15, MSG).

Because quietness is my ally when I try to study or write, I close my office door. It doesn't ensure silence, but dulls nearby conversations enough that they don't pique my interest. A note explains that I'm conserving quiet, but invites the visitor to pop in.

We might expect some places to be particularly quiet – such as certain libraries, museums, churches or wooded paths. But I didn't expect it of a greenhouse. My husband and I were staying in a rural area. He saw a hand-painted roadside sign advertising clocks and plants, so we stopped. While he made inquiries in the clock shop I looked around the sunny greenhouse. No one else was there. The only sounds were the soft tick of a clock and a gentle drip from recently watered hanging plants. I felt enveloped by peaceful quietness.

Today's Scripture advocates quietness and stillness as aids to our spiritual stability and victory: 'This is what the Sovereign LORD, the Holy One of Israel, says: "In repentance and rest is your salvation, in quietness and trust is your strength"' (v. 15).

Songwriter Darrell V. Archer sets it this way:

> Hush now, Christ waits for you;
> Hush now, his love is true.
> He died for your sin.
> Hush now, and let him in.
>
> Pray now, to God above;
> Pray now, for God is love.
> He'll hear your earnest plea,
> Pray now, he'll set you free.[28]

The Relax Reflex

'Then Jesus said, "Let's go off by ourselves to a quiet place and rest awhile"'
(Mark 6:31, NLT).

Our key verse almost slips out of sight between the stresses of an evangelistic campaign, John the Baptist's cruel death and the feeding of more than 5,000 people. The hoped-for respite doesn't come until late at night. Jesus sends the disciples across the lake, and then goes into the hills to pray. When Jesus comes their struggle ceases.

Mrs General Jean Brown reminds us:

It is common in these days to hear people say that we all live such busy and fast-moving lives that it is impossible to relax. Life's pace has accelerated, without doubt. Instead of taking three days to travel from Toronto to Vancouver, we do it in as many hours. This means less travel time for reflection, preparation or even relaxation.

Yehudi Menuhin, the world-famous violinist, has what he calls his Point Zero. After every tension, he says, he must return to the point of relaxation. Only by doing this continually, he feels, can one maintain a high level of activity and precision.

In violin playing, he says, two opposing muscles should never be tensed at the same time. 'We should always move from one to the other, allowing the one to recover while the other is being used,' Menuhin declares.

Let us make sure, then, that after the excitement of an occasion of superlative achievement, we may be able to return to Point Zero, for even a brief relaxation, so that the lovely music of dedicated service might continue.[29]

Relaxation counters tension and contributes an important role in maintaining a high level of musical precision. Returning to our point of spiritual rest and refreshment enables us to continue the particular Christian service the Lord calls each of us to offer.

Permeating Prayer

'But I have prayed for you, Simon, that your faith may not fail. And when you have turned back, strengthen your brothers' (Luke 22:32).

Yesterday we mentioned Christ's retreat to the hills after a very full day. General Albert Orsborn helpfully reminds us that as refreshing as spending time in natural settings might have been, ultimately that alone did not fortify Christ's spirit, nor will it ours:

Now, many servants of God go away into solitude; but it is not the wilderness, the quiet retreat that fortifies and reinforces the spirit – although silence itself is a wonderful restorative – but it is prayer in the silence that works wonders. Quietness of itself will not do us real good; it may even depress us by a revelation of inward poverty. It is prayer, much prayer, the true preparation for service that makes the difference.[30]

The Lord withdraws for prayer in preparation for ministry, for decisions, for his passion; but he also prays *after* service, teaching, opposition, misunderstanding. He requires solitude for intense communion with his Father and that intimate relationship permeates his life and ministry. It enables him to remain quiet under false accusation, rejection, disappointment, interruption, deprivation and when experiencing excruciating pain.

Consider Peter's denial, repentance and recommissioning we recently recalled. The way Jesus handled such personnel issues is instructive. Early day Salvation Army leader General Bramwell Booth's thoughts add a timely word. He writes of Jesus: 'He was as patient with those who left him as he was tender to those who were steadfast. He wants them with him, but goes forward without them in silence, love and expectation of restoration.'[31]

How can Jesus deal so firmly, kindly and hopefully with those closest to him who let him down? It can be no other way than by a prayer-permeated life. Such a way is open to each of his followers.

Quiet Strength

'Quiet down before GOD, be prayerful before him' (v. 7, MSG).

Mrs Commissioner Flora Larsson's poetry gives us spiritual insights in everyday living. Two excerpts from her prayer-poems ask God to help us know the great benefit that purposefully and regularly stilling ourselves in his presence brings. The first reflects on Revelation 8:1 when heaven falls silent.

In your Book the seer tells of silence in Heaven for what seemed
  half an hour.
Blest break in the celestial chanting,
welcome pause in the Heavenly harmonies:
A whole half hour . . . deep, satisfying silence,
something to look forward to
when earthly noise grates harshly on the ear.

In the meantime, Lord, help me to draw within myself,
stilling myself in the silence of my soul;
there finding strength and refreshing,
shut off from the world's jarring noises
for a few brief moments at a time.
A quiet oasis in a desert of sound.
there in that silence
I shall meet with you and again be strong.[32]

Help me, Lord, however difficult my circumstances,
to make some brief break of silence daily,
when I quiet myself before You,
think of your peace stealing into my heart,
rest in your love and rejoice in your goodness,
without uttering a word.
You will be there and know how to meet my need.[33]

Notes

1. Marlene Chase, *Our God Comes*, © 2000, Crest Books, The Salvation Army, USA.
2. *Beacon Bible Commentary, Vol. II*, © 1965, Beacon Hill Press of Kansas City, Kansas City, USA.
3. R. David Rightmire, *Sanctified Sanity: The Life and Teaching of Samuel Logan Brengle*, © 2003, Crest Books, The Salvation Army, USA.
4. Samuel Logan Brengle, *Helps to Holiness*, © 1912 The Salvation Army.
5. Wendy Lawton, *Impressions in Clay*, © 2005, Moody Publishers, Chicago, Illinois, USA.
6. Nell L. Kennedy, *Worthy Vessels*, © 1985, Zondervan Publishing House, Grand Rapids, Michigan, USA.
7. Shaw Clifton, *Never the Same Again*, © 1997, Crest Books, The Salvation Army, USA.
8. Darlene Zschech, 'The Potter's Hand', © 1993, Hillsong Publishing, Integrity's Hosanna! Music, Mobile, Alabama, USA.
9. Noel Hope, *Mildred Duff – A Surrendered Life*, © 1933, Salvationist Publishing and Supplies, London.
10. William Booth, *Purity of Heart*, first published 1902, revised edition 2007. © The Salvation Army.
11. Frederick Coutts, *The Call to Holiness*, © 1957, The Salvation Army.
12. William Booth, *Purity of Heart*, first published 1902, revised edition 2007. © The Salvation Army.
13. William Booth, *Purity of Heart*, first published 1902, revised edition 2007. © The Salvation Army.
14. A. F. Kirkpatrick, *The Cambridge Bible for Schools and Colleges: The Book of Psalms, Books IV and V, Psalms XC-CL*, © 1903, C. J. Clay and Sons, Cambridge University Press.
15. Quoted by W. Stewart McCullough, *The Interpreter's Bible, Vol. IV*, ed. George A. Buttrick, © 1955, Abingdon Press, New York, USA.
16. Larry Smith and Rachel Fershleiser's compilation, *Not Quite What I Was Planning – Six-word Memoirs*, © 2008. HarperCollins Publishers, New York, USA.
17. A. F. Kirkpatrick, *The Cambridge Bible for Schools and Colleges: The Book of Psalms, Books IV and V, Psalms XC-CL*, © 1903, C. J. Clay and Sons, Cambridge University Press.

18. Joseph Alexander Addison, *The Psalms Translated and Explained. Vol. 2*, sixth edition, 1873, © Scribner, Armstrong & Co., New York, USA.

19. *Adult Faith Connections Bible Study Guide*, © 2009, WordAction Publishing Company, Kansas City, Missouri, USA.

20. From the CD *The Greatest Adventure, A Spiritual Journey in Poetry and Song with Keith and Pauline Banks*. © 2008 Radiovision Networks, Largs, Scotland.

21. Peter M. Cooke, set to the tune 'Tell Me, Lovely Shepherd', by William Boyce; published in *The Musical Salvationist*, October 1978, © Salvationist Publishing & Supplies Ltd.

22. Donald W. Richardson, *The Revelation of Jesus Christ*, © 1964, John Knox Press, Richmond, Virginia, USA.

23. William Barclay, *The Daily Study Bible Series: The Gospel of John, vol. 1*, St Andrew Press, Edinburgh, 1955, revised and updated, 1975.

24. *Psalms 90–150: The Interpreter's Bible, Vol. IV*, ed. George Buttrick, © 1955, Abingdon Press, New York, USA.

25. Arthur John Gossip, 'The Gospel According to St John', *The Interpreter's Bible, Vol. VIII*, ed. George A. Buttrick *et al.*, © 1952, Abingdon-Cokesbury Press, New York, USA.

26. Peter M. Cooke, *Pilgrims – Selections from Salvationist Poets*, © 1988, The Salvation Army.

27. Madeleine L'Engle, *A Circle of Quiet*, © 1971, Farrar, Straus & Giroux, New York, USA.

28. Darrell V. Archer, 'Hush Now', © 1973, Main Stream Music, Carol Stream, Illinois, USA, used by permission.

29. Jean Brown, *Excursions in Thought*, © 1980, The Salvation Army.

30. Albert Orsborn, *The Silences of Christ*, © 1954, The Salvation Army.

31. Bramwell Booth, *Our Master*, © 1908, The Salvation Army.

32. *Just a Moment, Lord*, Flora Larsson, © 1973, Hodder & Stoughton, London, UK.

33. *God in my Everyday*, Flora Larsson, © 1984, Hodder & Stoughton, London, UK.

Index

1 Peter	September–December 2008
2 Peter	January–April 2007
1 John	January–April 2011
2, 3 John	September–December 2006
	May–August 2010
Jude	September–December 2009

Subscribe...

Words of Life is published three times a year:
January–April, May–August and September–December

Four easy ways to subscribe

- By post – simply complete and return the subscription form below
- By phone – +44 (0)1933 445 445
- By email – mail_order@sp-s.co.uk
- Or visit your local Christian bookshop

SUBSCRIPTION FORM

Name (Miss, Mrs, Ms, Mr)...

Address ....

....

.... Postcode ....

Tel. No..

Email* ....

Annual Subscription Rates
UK £10.50   *Non-UK* £10.50 + £3.90 P&P = £14.40
Please send me .... copy/copies of the next three issues of *Words of Life* commencing with **May 2011**

Total: £ .... **I enclose payment by cheque** ☐
Please make cheques payable to *The Salvation Army*

Please debit my Access/Mastercard/Visa/American Express/Switch card

Card No. ☐☐☐☐ ☐☐☐☐ ☐☐☐☐ ☐☐☐☐   Expiry date: ___ /___

Security No. ☐☐☐   **Issue number (Switch only)** _____

Cardholder's signature: .... Date: ....

Please send this form and any cheques to: **The Mail Order Department, Salvationist Publishing and Supplies, 66–78 Denington Road, Denington Industrial Estate, Wellingborough, Northamptonshire NN8 2QH, UK**

☐ *We would like to keep in touch with you by placing you on our mailing list. If you would prefer not to receive correspondence from us, please tick this box. The Salvation Army does not sell or lease its mailing lists.